WILLIAM ALPHAEUS HUNTON

HUNTON

A Pioneer Prophet
of Young Men

by

ADDIE W. HUNTON

ASSOCIATION PRESS

347 Madison Avenue   New York

1938

PRINTED IN THE UNITED STATES OF AMERICA

TO THE MANY YOUNG MEN
WHO KNEW MR. HUNTON'S INFLUENCE
SO WELL IN THE PAST
AND
TO THE MANY MORE YOUNG MEN
WHO WILL CONTINUE TO FEEL IT
IN THE FUTURE

Foreword

THE TITLE of this book is apt. William A. Hunton was distinctly a pioneer and pathfinder. His life at every stage was one of adventure.

He was a foundation layer. Although many of successive generations may participate in raising the superstructure, only a greatly favored few are privileged to lay the foundation of a beneficent institution or movement. The foundation he laid was broad and deep and solid. The materials he employed were enduring and proved capable of sustaining great weight. He not only pioneered a great youth movement, but, as has been pointed out by a discerning observer, "he remained with it long enough to determine its character and to insure beyond peradventure its continuance."

He was also a real leader. The marks of the true leader are that he knows the way, keeps ahead, and has the gift of contagion that influences others to follow him. Think of the scope of his leadership. He influenced the youth of the Negro race of America, both South and North; he planted societies in all the important Negro colleges and likewise in many of the major cities of the land; his following embraced members of all denominations and transcended party lines; his ideas and principles commanded the acceptance and enlisted the support of the men of standing and influence of the white race. What characterized his leadership? A clear sense of direction and mission; the employment of sound guiding principles; open-mindedness and broad-mindedness; courage; self-effacement; unusual poise, patience, and perseverance; heart power; and the ability to co-operate.

He was a prophet. He lived on the mountains. He was a man of vision. In thought and plan he exercised foresight and moved in large dimensions. This helps to explain his power with youth. It accounts for the remarkable group of workers of the constructive, altruistic forces of his race who are indebted to him for their life vision and life dedication. As a prophet he fearlessly declared warfare against evils of his day and faithfully warned against alarming perils. In a day of inflamed race relations he helped to usher in a period of conciliation, good will, and brotherhood.

It is well that we have this worthy record of one of the group of gifted forerunners of a great race. It has its message of hope, encouragement, and guidance for the oncoming, ambitious youth of the black race of America and Africa, and likewise for the youth of the white race. The talented and devoted writer has accomplished her work of love with fine restraint and discerning, sympathetic insight.

JOHN R. MOTT

New York, June, 1938

Preface

I HAVE penned the closing chapters of this book with a keen awareness that the twenty-two years since the passing of Mr. Hunton are but as yesterday. He stamped his personality deeply not only on the two and a half generations of young people whom he so loyally and lovingly served, but he gathered a profound respect and devotion from the many different channels of life into which his work flowed.

Wherever I have moved since his "Great Adventure" there has been an insistent demand that the facts of his life be recorded for authentic future reference.

I had first to adjust myself for the very difficult task of evaluating Mr. Hunton impersonally as a man rather than as a devoted husband and comrade for many years. It was necessary to come to the realization of the fact that his value to his times and to posterity was not merely in the undisputed fineness of his character, however impressive that may have been, but more exactly in his permanent influence through the great movement with which he was so long associated. There has never been any doubt that there should be an impersonal study of his twenty-five years of service, to test the value of his activities in permanently imbedding the fundamental principles of the Young Men's Christian Association in the lives of the youth of his race.

Before such a task could be undertaken, it was necessary that time should pass, and, as it seemed decreed, surcease for my loss and pain found in work on the battle-torn soil of France. In the intervening years I have re-read hundreds of letters that had their beginning three years before our marriage and that continued twenty years after. They are the very precious documents, first of a wooer, and then of a devoted husband. They are very human, and in them I have found revealed, with an intimacy unequaled elsewhere in his writings—the heart throbs, the patience, the dauntless courage of a crusader.

ix

In Canada, among the scenes of his childhood and early manhood, I have conversed with his boyhood friends and with some aged friends of his father's day. Most of all I talked with his brothers and sisters and gathered information from them. Especially am I indebted to the late Victoria Hunton Berry, who was not only a devoted sister but the only mother he ever really knew, faithful unto his death. While rearing him, she placed upon him the seal of her own sweet and cheerful spirit.

As far as possible, I have let his own words and those of his associates unfold Mr. Hunton's life. There were few, if any, spectacular or dramatic pictures in it. However, covering as it did, comparatively, but a short span of years, it was full and rich to overflowing—ever stirring, ever expanding.

Many years before Mr. Hunton's death, Dr. W. E. B. DuBois referred to him as "A Pioneer Prophet of Young Men"—and because I have never been able to find another term that could apply quite so appropriately and exquisitely to him, I am indebted for permission to use it as the subtitle of this book, as I am also for the use of quotations herein found. Most of all, perhaps, I am indebted to that loving friend, Violet Johnson, in whose home at beautiful Summit, New Jersey—away from the din of the City— I found the seclusion and quiet needed to write this book.

That Mr. Hunton visioned the future with prophetic eye is attested to in the present status of the Association Movement. In the very blood and tissues of his being he was a pioneer—he is one of those "Who have gone where none before had dared and earned new advantages and comforts for their brothers." He "made new roads, where before no roads existed."

A. W. H.

Contents

CHRONOLOGY

1843   Stanton Hunton, father of William Alphaeus Hunton, settled at Chatham, Ontario.

1858   Stanton Hunton met John Brown and became associated with him in his preparations for the Harper's Ferry attack.

1863   William Alphaeus Hunton born at Chatham.

1883   Became a public-school teacher.

1885   Entered government service at Ottawa.

1888   Went to Norfolk, Virginia, as first employed Y.M.C.A. secretary for work among colored men.

1891   Became the first colored secretary of the staff of the International Committee of the Y.M.C.A.'s.

1892   Wrote *First Steps*, a pamphlet that attained wide circulation.

1892   Met for the first time Mr. J. E. Moorland. The beginning of a life-long association and friendship.

1893   Married at Norfolk, Virginia.

1894   Delegate to the Y.M.C.A. Golden Jubilee Convention in London, England.

1898   Worked among soldiers in the Army camps during the Spanish-American War.

1898   Joined by Mr. Moorland on the staff of the International Committee of the Y.M.C.A.'s.

1907   Attended World's Student Christian Federation Conference in Tokyo.

1910   Mr. Julius Rosenwald's liberal offer to colored Y.M.C.A.'s heralds a new era.

1913   Led colored delegation to World's Student Christian Federation Conference at Lake Mohonk, New York.

1914   Began preparation for Negro Student Congress.

1914   Stricken by illness. Took up residence at Saranac Lake, New York.

1915   Returned to New York City.

1916   Died at Brooklyn, New York.

xii

CHAPTER ONE

Pioneer Influences

1843-1863

"THE UNDERGROUND RAILROAD" is a most thrilling and authentic story of the attempt of hundreds of slaves who dared, even in the face of death, to risk the chance to escape from a cruel and wholly pernicious system. Slavery, more often dehumanizing to both master and mastered than otherwise, had overspread the nation like a black cloud that grew more and more ominous with time and, by its very character, united the spirit, influence, and power of real humanitarians. These humanitarians made up the unseen force that gave strength and effectiveness to the work of the Underground Railroad.

The Fugitive Slave Law, passed in 1793, made living in the North insecure for slaves who had escaped. In 1818, its teeth were sharpened by drastic amendments. The severity of the Compromise Law in regard to slavery in 1850—which was but another step toward the crisis—made the security of the fugitive slave in the North most precarious. The Underground Railroad was forced to find a direct route across the border into Canada; the Province of Ontario became the desired haven, and some seventy thousand fugitive slaves had found their way there by the middle of the nineteenth century.

Just eleven miles north of Lake Erie, in western Ontario, was a rich agricultural district, well adapted to fruit growing, that had fallen into the hands of the English about 1759. At the beginning of the nineteenth century it had been unbroken wilderness with roving Indians, although in 1795 six hundred acres for a town plot had been set aside by the Governor of the province. There was no real settlement there until 1830, when William Chrysler, the first white settler, built a log hut. Because of the variety of fine timber and the agricultural advantages, the settlement grew very rapidly. In 1831 a school house was built, and by 1833 the population numbered six hundred. The settlement was named Chatham, and the little river that flowed through it, and which had been called Escunispe by the Indians and La France during the French domination, was named The Thames—all in honor of the homeland across the ocean.

The advantages of this fertile region reached the ears of fugitive slaves, and to this "Promised Land" many of them made their way straight from down in "Egypt Land." Among those who found this haven was Stanton Hunton, who became one of the rugged settlers of Chatham and who was destined to be the father of our pioneer prophet.

Stanton Hunton had made three ineffectual attempts to run away to freedom, and each effort had left him more determined to escape. He was the slave of a most humane maiden lady of the Virginia aristocracy, bound to her not only by ties of slavery but by those of blood. She liked him very much and quite surreptitiously assisted his education from early childhood, so that he grew up an unusually intelligent youth. But his owner would not permit him to buy his freedom—the thing he most craved, often plead for, and strove vainly to secure. Writing me from Erie, Pa., on the occasion of his first visit there, my husband said, "I wish I could find the site of the hotel at which my father stopped in one of his efforts to escape from slavery, and where he was caught and rudely returned to Virginia." Realizing the difficulty of holding him, his owner finally permitted Stanton Hunton to buy himself. The purchase was accomplished about 1840, and he left Virginia, stopped in Washington for a short while, and, with help, cautiously made his way to Canada and finally to Chatham.

But he was not altogether satisfied with obtaining his own freedom, and so, after pioneering for a year or so, he made his way again far enough into the United States to negotiate for the freedom of his brother Ben, who was then a slave in Natchez, Mississippi. This effort was successful, and his brother returned to Chatham with him, but soon succumbed to the severity of the life and climate. Stanton Hunton found himself overcome with loneliness and decided to go once again to Cincinnati, where he had seen many lovely colored girls, and there seek for devotion and companionship. He was wholly successful, and married Mary Ann Conyer, a beautiful Cincinnati girl, and with her returned to Chatham to make their home. No doubt he was filled with the happy visions of a young and loving husband as well as the aspiration of a stalwart pioneer, but probably did not dream that his little town of Chatham, which he was so enthusiastically helping to develop, would in a few years acquire widespread fame. About 1845, attempts were made to have Chatham recognized as the capital of the Province of Ontario, but that honor was given to Toronto. However, the glory with which Chatham became invested, because of its relation to John Brown in one of the most tragic episodes of American history, still endures. It marks the little town as an important spot to the thousands of men and women who have placed the name of that fervid humanitarian in the galaxy of world martyrs.

In 1858, John Brown found his way to Ontario, where so many ex-slaves had located. He visited Toronto and other towns in that area, and finally reached Chatham. After conference with Martin R. Delaney and other prominent colored men, he decided to make Chatham the base of his preparations for the first onslaught to be made against that great American octopus, human slavery. Chatham was centrally located and had an intelligent citizenry, and close to it was the Negro settlement of Buxton, which had been founded in 1848 by the Reverend William King with fifteen freed slaves as a nucleus. That settlement had grown rapidly, and after ten years was thickly populated.

John Brown had confided his real purpose to but few persons, and they had agreed to keep it secret until he could make a trip to the States and return. Among those in his confidence besides Martin R. Delaney were Isaac Holden, J. M. Jones, and Stanton Hunton. He then made a hurried trip to the United States, and on April 29, 1858, returned to Chatham with those brave leaders who were to follow him even unto death. With them he at once began the consummation of his plans for the attack at Harper's Ferry.

The next three weeks were very busy ones. A temporary organization was formed, with the Reverend W. C. Monroe as president

3

and John Brown as commander-in-chief. Many meetings and conferences were held, some in the church and some in the homes of Isaac Holden and Stanton Hunton. At this time John Brown was the guest of Isaac Holden, whose daughter, Belle, was later to marry Ben, the oldest son of Stanton Hunton.

On May 5, 1858, three days before the final convention, John Brown sent out the following terse call:

My Dear Friend:

I have called a quiet conference in this place, May 8, and your attendance is earnestly requested.

Your friend,
JOHN BROWN

Stanton Hunton was one of the very quiet but earnest members of the group that met May 8, 1858, in Fire Engine House Number Three, which had been built by Isaac Holden. One member of the Conference wrote: "There was scant ceremony at these opening proceedings by these earnest men. They were of two colors but one mind and all were equal in degree and station here. No civic address to this Canadian town; no beat of drums; no firing of guns was heard. The place was rude and unadorned, yet the object of this little parliament was the freedom of four million slaves."

A table at which John Brown sat and wrote has been preserved in the Hunton family; but the Hunton homestead at King and Wellington Streets, known still as "Hunton's Corner," is the present site of the depot of the Canadian Pacific Railroad, for which purpose it was sold by Mr. Hunton. However, the later Hunton home and the Holden home still stand, plain but sturdy and dignified, like their early owners.

It was my privilege, when a bride, to be a guest in Mr. Holden's home and to meet the tall, handsome old man who was probably John Brown's largest Chatham contributor of time, service, and money. Although a very old man when I met him, he was still keen in his memory of the scenes and events in Chatham at that important period that thrilled to the dynamic power of John Brown.

It was into this environment, so rich in its pioneer influences,

4

strong humanitarian principles, and Christian faith that, on October 31, 1863, Stanton Hunton's sixth son, William Alphaeus Hunton, was born. He was to inherit not only the pioneer and far-visioned qualities involved in this background, but also the quiet, reticent, but stalwart character of his father and the grace and charm of a mother who had died too early for him to really know her and who would be to him all his life but a beautiful dream.

CHAPTER TWO

Early Life in Canada

1863-1885

THE LIFE work of William A. Hunton was not chosen by accident. He finally entered upon it with a knowledge, vision, and spirit gained only by years of preparation through the faithful performance of duties assigned to his hands.

Back of that first and very happy experience in Association work at Ottawa; back of his meeting with some members of the staff of the International Committee; far back of that humble prayer circle at Norfolk, Virginia, discovered in 1887 by a visiting Englishman who recognized its potentialities—back of all these were the tradition and training that made possible a favorable reaction to the later influences upon his life.

One great writer has said that "Traditions of ancient honor impart something of their dignity to those who inherit them." Inextricably woven into the very nature of William A. Hunton was the unusual and inspiring tradition of his forbears—a tradition that included a new-born hope resulting from the Emancipation Proclamation, signed only a short time prior to his birth.

His training was fortunately placed in careful and loving hands. He was born into a free and intelligent atmosphere, as one of a large and happy family. His mother died when he was about four years old, and his memory of her was based rather on images of her painted by the family than on any definite knowledge. His home had the supervision of a fine Christian father, a loving sister, and, for a time, a stern but devoted maternal grandmother. He had six brothers, all except one of whom were older than he; and, in addition to the older sister, Victoria, there was a cherished younger sister Mary. He had many pals, all full of the abundant life of youth. Some of his childhood friends I have met in manhood: their devotion still remained sincere and deep, with an added pride and respect for their "Billie." This was the name given him by one and all in those early associations, and it was a name that he dearly loved his intimates to use. In our early married life, he tried to teach me to call him by that name, but, although I made an earnest effort, I failed. The fact was that here in the United States, where I had met and known him, he was always called "Mr. Hunton" or else "Hunton"; and my visits to the bosom of his family were too rare and too brief for me to become accustomed to this more intimate name.

His father believed that boys should be systematically industrious, so that in those days, when lamps had to be prepared for lighting, wood cut both for heating and cooking, floors and yards swept, snow cleaned away in season, and countless errands performed because there were not telephones, each child had his work. Mr. Hunton has humorously told how, if chores ran short, his father would keep his boys busy by having changed from one section of the yard to another the huge pile of brick that he kept on hand as a brick-mason. For a time the father had a store and a hall, the management of which he left largely to his sons in addition to their school duties and regular chores. Thus his father implanted in him very early in his life the habit of industriousness that proved a valuable asset to him in his later busy life.

Stanton Hunton was not only a Christian, but he had a fixed faith in religious tradition and custom, and would, if need be, vigorously defend that faith against any admixture of newer theories or "isms." He held all his children to religious observance, but it was William who most deeply felt and practised the Christian graces of his father, so that he was dubbed by his brothers "the parson." In his early youth he became a Christian and taught the men's Bible class in his Sunday School. His own father was a member of this class.

William A. Hunton was given the best educational advantages of his time; he finished high school, and later, after a four years' course, graduated from the Wilberforce Institute of Ontario. On our first visit together to his beloved Canada, he took me to call on one of his former school principals. The old gentleman put his arms around Mr. Hunton most affectionately and with a laughing seriousness said, "Billie was not a genius but he was even better—a fine, honest student, and I always felt that some day we would be proud of him."

He had a very real but quiet sense of humor that was never obvious to strangers, but which his intimates knew and delighted in. Once in a literary society of which he was a member, he and his closest friend were each assigned the task of writing papers. In some mysterious way he gained possession of his pal's paper, copied it *verbatim*, and asked the privilege of giving his own essay first. Very gravely he proceeded to read while his friend sitting on the front seat grew more and more restless and finally jumped to his feet exclaiming, "Mr. President, Billie has stolen my paper!" This ended not only Billie's gravity but the dignity of the session. He was promptly fined twenty-five cents and silenced for a time. But even in later years, whenever he met this dear friend, he enjoyed greatly teasing him about that early joke.

Mr. Hunton had a great fondness for apples of any kind, even dried apples, which he constantly and humorously filched from the family's winter supply, and thus earned the added title of "Billie-dried-apples." His very first question to me about my culinary ability was not if I could make bread or cake, but if I knew how to make an apple cobbler. As I had never before heard of it, he began with great earnestness to tell me how his sister prepared it. I had to learn by experience that his recipe, though presumably given with honest intentions, was more largely a concoction of his own brain than that of his sister. But I did learn to know that a good apple cobbler or pie was a real remedy for many of his ills.

Mr. Hunton grew to manhood with that rare wit and good humor that was to prove exceedingly helpful in a career crowded with perplexing problems. I often felt that he and Mr. J. E. Moorland, with whom he was so closely associated for two decades, were frequently able to find themselves "smiling through" because their humor was so akin, and because of the real enjoyment they could find in practising it upon each other.

The first work to which our pioneer prophet was called was that of teacher. It was in the public school of the little town of Dresden, Canada, near his home town, that he had his first and

8

last experience as master of a schoolroom. This work was not undertaken as a choice, but as his first opportunity. He was anxious to get into a larger field, where he might have opportunity to study for the ministry, and it was with this in mind that, soon after he began to teach, he took an examination for a government position at Ottawa. It was ordained that his teaching days should not be long, for he soon received the following communication from the clerk of Privy Council at Ottawa:

Certified Extract from the Minutes of a Meeting of the Treasury Board held on the 4th of May 1885, approved by His Excellency the Governor General in Council on the 11th of May, 1885.

Indian Affairs:

That Mr. William A. Hunton, who has passed the necessary qualifying Examination, be appointed a probationary clerk in the Department of Indian Affairs at a salary of $1,000 per annum.

He resigned his school work with some alacrity, and never went back to it again, although he said in later years that even teaching at Dresden had been, in several distinct ways, an important part of his education.

From the time of his conversion in early youth he had felt the urge to prepare for strictly Christian service. He had been encouraged in this by the minister under whom he was so early converted, and who, no doubt, from that time until his death remained his closest spiritual adviser and one of his closest friends: the Reverend J. Albert Johnson, afterward Bishop Johnson, and with whom Mr. Hunton, no matter how long nor how widely separated, kept in close contact through a correspondence that was helpful and inspiring to both of them. Later in life Bishop Johnson, who was a fine scholar, wrote letters, while on his mission field in South Africa, to his friend "Willie," that were in themselves epics, and which profoundly stirred his spiritual heroism.

One of the many fine letters from the Rev. Johnson reads as follows:

9

My dear Willie:

It is Sunday night. I am alone in my study—the day's work is over. I am full of thoughts—as to the result—I have sown—the Master will see that the seed grows—My congregation was very large tonight—my text Matt. 9-9, "Follow Me." The Lord was with us. Ah Me! how comforting the thought. It seems strange that you are so much in my thoughts lately.

A few of the thoughts suggested by my text tonight, will perhaps be worth your consideration:—What did Matthew leave to "follow" Christ? His *occupation.* (Not his property.) His *Spiritual errors.* His *sinful worldliness,* etc. What did he gain? A *change of occupation.*—(Recorder of the incidents and gospel of Christ). *Peace of heart* and *conscience* —A *Friend. Qualification* for and *opportunities* of usefulness in the divine life—The *goodly inheritance* and *eternal life.*

So I think when He says to us of today "Follow Me" it is to active useful life—You may say, "It is not clear where and how I am to go"—where does your prayerful and meditative spirit prompt you to go? Could you be induced to go into foreign missionary life in the West Indies? A great field and "white unto harvest." Of course you would go under different circumstances than *our* early missionaries went. You would be sure of temporal support.

Or would you take work in the South of this continent, and there in our ministry proclaim the "glorious Gospel," which "is worthy of all acceptation," to our people? I long to see you in the ministry telling the wondrous story, to which work I have long been persuaded the Master would have you go. And but for the unfortunate circumstances arising out of the Union with the A. M. E. Church, I trow not, you would have been today. In the appealed case, the decision of Judge Proudfoot has been affirmed, so that the outlook of a speedy settlement is not promising—but the Church belongs to God. I do not despair—all that is in danger is not lost—has frequently in my own observation been proven. The questions you ask—I will answer on another night than Sunday.

Think over my proposals—and in the mean time write me. I seem dissatisfied if I do not hear from you often nowadays. Speak as freely to me as you wish in confidence on any subject.

Accept our love, interest, and best wishes.

Believe me your
friend and brother
J. A. JOHNSON

When Mr. Hunton went to Ottawa he had the earnest intention of preparing eventually for specific Christian service. After finding a good family with whom to live, his next step was to join the Church and the Young Men's Christian Association. In these he became enthusiastically active; he was a member of both the choir and of the Sunday-school staff in the large white congregation at Ottawa, as he had been in his own little church in Chatham. He was perhaps the only colored member of the Young Men's Christian Association, but constantly advanced in usefulness and in honor, becoming the chairman of the Boys' Work Department. Among his most precious possessions was a library—one book from each boy—presented by that department when he left for the United States in 1888.

In all his relationships at Ottawa, Mr. Hunton was very happy, and in many respects it was the most ideally satisfying period of his life. And yet he was not completely satisfied there. He still longed for the service that would answer his soul's chief desire to be altogether used by the Master for the spread of his kingdom here on earth. He may have found patience and faith in a dim awareness, at least, that all of his fine opportunities at Ottawa were giving him strength and knowledge for that future of which he dreamed.

We know that he was destined to go into the Southland as God's minister to men, but that he would go through one of the agencies of the Church rather than through the Church directly. He would penetrate to the very heart of an untried field and become the first Negro apostle of the Young Men's Christian Association. It would be God's will finding fulfillment in the life of the Young Men's Christian Association and in the life of this pioneer prophet.

CHAPTER THREE

The Call and the Answer

1885-1888

VARIOUS processes set themselves to work at Chatham, Ontario, to make a rhythmic pattern of William A. Hunton's life. Later, in Ottawa, where he had gone merely as a government clerk, his environment and his own steadfastness to his ideals made possible the further enrichment and value of that pattern. He was peculiarly sensitive to all spiritual beauty and had an unabashed joy in the service of the Master, radiating it with such force that those who touched him realized its sincerity and strength.

While he was being fitted for the mission to which he would presently be called out into the world, a certain vague uneasiness and nebulous convictions were stirring in the hearts of men that would finally take definite form and somehow unite Mr. Hunton to the cause that would gain his life's utter devotion.

It is best to let Mr. Hunton himself speak from these pages about those days when humanitarian principles were stirring and convictions were growing in the Young Men's Christian Association relative to its duty to colored men. Early in his Association career he spent time in gathering facts about the movement that went back through the years as far as his own infancy and which, for the first time had correlation through his efforts. He had heard of the sporadic organization, about 1866, in South Carolina, North Carolina, Washington, and other places; of the splendid efforts of Mr. Eato, about that same period, to organize an Association for colored men in New York City, and of his plea before the International Convention held at Montreal, for the inclusion of men of his race in the Association Movement. Mr. Hunton also knew that at that same Convention General O. O.

Howard and others had introduced resolutions in support of Mr. Eato's plea.

In 1892 Mr. Hunton wrote as follows:

It is known that as early as 1870 there were attempts to organize the Young Men's Christian Associations in many Southern cities and towns by colored men, but receiving no assistance from those who understood the principles and methods of the work, these soon proved fruitless. Nothing practically was done for this large class of our population until the International Convention held at Richmond, Virginia, in 1875. This was the first International Convention held in the South after the Civil War. At this Convention there was one colored delegate, a student from Howard University —Robert Wheeler, now an outstanding minister in the Congregational Church. So deeply did the colored ministers of Richmond feel the need of some special effort in behalf of colored young men, that they sent in a petition asking the Convention to pray that God would open the way for the extension of Association work among our young men in the South. This petition was received with great enthusiasm and, before prayer was offered, Major Joseph Hardie of Selma, Alabama, President of the Convention, said, "There is a great work to be done among the colored people of the South. I speak from experience when I tell you that there is a wide field opening to us, and we are called upon to take up this work." At the Toronto Convention in 1876 this subject was again considered, the delegates, particularly from the South, urging that the International Committee be authorized to undertake the extension of the work to this new field. This was done and Mr. Henry E. Brown became Secretary of the International Committee for work among colored men. He gave about twelve years of fruitful service, principally among students.

In 1886, while Mr. Hunton was in Ottawa, he came under the observation of some members of the staff of the International Committee of the Y.M.C.A., and information about him found its way to the New York headquarters. He was handsome, cultured, and very definitely earnest. Inquiries were made relative to his availability for work among colored men of the South, but it seems that Mr. Hunton was not quite ready for a decision, knowing so little of the field to which he would be called. Corre-

13

spondence on the subject lagged for a time, but the whole question came to a focus in 1887. Mr. Joseph Smithson, an Englishman, visiting Norfolk, Virginia, at that time, discovered a prayer circle of colored young men and became greatly interested in it. He wrote to the International Committee with such enthusiasm and faith in the possibilities of this group for a real city Association that the Committee became deeply interested. It sent Mr. H. E. Brown, who then had the national supervision of colored work, to co-operate with Mr. Smithson.

Mr. Kuhring, the General Secretary of the Ottawa Association, in which Mr. Hunton was very active, had become not only his close friend but was aware of his effort to find a place of usefulness in Christian service among his own people. He was anxious to have him used in Association work and had resumed correspondence on the subject.

Mr. Richard C. Morse, Executive Secretary of the International Committee, wrote Mr. Kuhring in September, 1887, as follows:

Mr. Kuhring.
My Dear Friend:—

Your letter to Mr. Ingersoll was referred to me and brought to the attention of the Committee at its meeting last night. I recall the former correspondence concerning Mr. Hunton. The impression left upon our mind by our failing to get a reply to our last inquiry was that something had interfered with Mr. Hunton's seriously considering the matter further at that time. We are very glad to re-open correspondence upon it, and the Committee wants to do all in its power to facilitate such an excellent work on the part of Mr. Hunton as you suggest.

I do not wonder that you value him and would be very slow to have him leave Ottawa, but I agree with you that if a field is opened to him at the South he could accomplish vastly more there for his race. The most serious question raised by the Committee was whether Mr. Hunton was intelligently aware of the social sacrifices that might be involved in his undertaking things very different there from what they are at Ottawa, in the way of his social intercourse with white and colored people alike, and the change would involve trial and self-sacrifice on his part. But probably he has been in the South and understands all this.

The Committee, however, thought that it would be wise for him have correspondence with Mr. H. E. Brown, our Secretary, who has been engaged in work in behalf of and among colored young men for the last twenty years, and who is in a position to confer with Mr. Hunton and make intelligible to him the present situation at the South and the circumstances under which such work as you proposed for him would be attempted. So I have instructed Mr. Brown to open correspondence with you and Mr. Hunton upon this subject. For some time we have been desirous of beginning a colored department of our work in some of the large cities at the South and in such connection with the existing Associations as you suggest. When your letter came we were planning for a trip by Mr. Brown at the South to such cities as give most promise of being able to organize such a work in connection with existing Associations there. So your letter is a very providential help, and I am hopeful that Mr. Hunton may prove to be just the man to become the first colored secretary at the South, a leader and fore-runner of many more. But, as you will readily understand, this is a matter in which we must proceed carefully and with less rapidity than we would like.

Soon after this Mr. Brown wrote to Mr. Kuhring:

Dear Brother:

A copy of yours of 8/24 to Mr. Ingersoll is sent me. Do you know whether Mr. Hunton would now be glad to go South as General Secretary? Does he realize the very different relation he must in the South bear to the white folk from that which he now bears? Is he sufficiently consecrated to endure the change? Does he know what salary he would accept? How much education has he?

From this point the correspondence seems to have gone forward between Mr. Brown and Mr. Hunton alone to its final results. Again Mr. Brown wrote early in December, 1887:

Friend Hunton:

I have just reached home and find your letter awaiting me. The International Committee is not in the habit of employing men as they go to their fields to engage in the work of General Secretary. I have done what I could toward opening the way for you in Norfolk, just as I do for other men in other fields. I shall be glad to make another trip to Norfolk to complete the preparation for the opening of the work among the colored people, and I hoped that you would find a large field of usefulness, but I cannot promise that the International Committee will secure your salary till you enter the work as General Secretary.

I will, however, pledge you that your traveling expenses from Ottawa to Norfolk shall be met by some one, and if there should be any failure on the part of the Norfolk people to arrange with you at $800 a year, I will either find another field for you or will secure for you your return traveling expenses. I understand of course that there is some risk, but it seems to me very small.

I did not expect you to have much to do with the securing of subscriptions, but did suppose that you would like to plan with us in regard to the reorganization of the Association and selection of rooms, etc.

If anything should happen to prevent the consummation of our plans in Norfolk, there are several larger cities in that region. But I have no idea of a failure.

Yours in haste so as to reach the next train.

Then, December 15, Mr. Brown wrote the letter below:

Friend Hunton:

I reached Norfolk (one of the points where I hoped you could be secured) last Saturday. Mr. Smithson was there, and had gotten your name from New York and has now rec'd your letter.

It seemed to be of the Lord that my visit should occur while Mr. Smithson is there and after we had begun to talk of a full colored work. I met the colored Association twice and started our ball rolling. We raised in Subscriptions $35 per month toward the work among the fifty young men present Mon. night. Much work will be required to collect this money and some of it will doubtless fail, but there are a *good many* leading colored people to be seen personally and some white people. Mr. Smithson has offered to double all that the colored people raise up to $400—i.e., if they raise $400 or less he will make it $800 or less, he giving as much as they give. I now expect to return to Norfolk early in January to complete the preparations already begun for a full work in rented rooms, for the colored people of Norfolk. Of course I expect to get you located there as General Secretary.

I think it very important that you be there with me and take part in the effort to secure the money, rooms, etc., and especially to help in getting the right men on the board of managers.

They have an Association already, but are ready to reorganize so far as may seem necessary in order to adapt themselves to the larger field which they are to occupy. It is a little awkward for a man to go to such a field before he is regularly called to it, but I think I can adjust such matters so as not to annoy anyone. Can you possible leave Ottawa on so short notice? If necessary I *might* defer my visit to Norfolk till about the *middle* of January instead of making it earlier.

Write me immediately as to your thought in this matter. I will write you soon again, probably this week.

This brought a decisive reply from Hunton, who wired: "Can reach Norfolk January 10 on conditions of letter now sending."

That message involved a momentous decision. Mr. Hunton knew that his entire family was quite skeptical as to the wisdom of his decision. They had anticipated his entry into the ministry, but had scant knowledge of the field he had now chosen. To them it was as if he were going to the heart of darkest Africa, and, while withholding any opposition, they were anxious and unreconciled to this plunge into an unknown and very new field. His friend, the Rev. Albert Johnson, felt sure that "Willie" was called to and needed in the Christian ministry. His friends in the Department of Indian Affairs, where he worked, believed he would soon return and refused to accept his resignation immediately, simply giving him a leave of absence. He himself was torn between his desire for the unknown, with his pioneer spirit urging him on, and his desire to keep the love and companionship at hand in Ottawa and all it had to offer.

But he did answer the call and reached Norfolk early in January, 1888. He said to me many times during his active years and in days when his sun was gradually setting: "I really had no choice. It was God's leading and I could but follow." Just before leaving Ottawa, he wrote in a precious little book: "Dear old Ottawa, I shall never forget the three years I have spent here among the Chelsea Hills."

By the time he reached Norfolk a letter awaited him reading thus:

Young Men's Christian Association
Ottawa, 12th Jany. 1888

Dear Mr. Hunton,

The Board desire to convey to you their regret at your removal from their midst. They wish to place on record their appreciation of your ability, self-denial, and perseverance, in your labor of love, on behalf of the boys, as well as your kind assistance in many of the projects which the Board saw fit to devise. They would convey at same time their earnest wish that you may be used of God in your new field, as you have been in Ottawa. They will always look upon your work with interest, as you have won their affections.

Yours sincerely,
JAMES GIBSON,
President

Much would happen before he would revisit his beloved Ottawa.

CHAPTER FOUR

Testing Years

1888-1891

THE YEAR 1888 dawned with a high importance and a high expectancy of new and positive advantages for colored men in their relationship with the Young Men's Christian Association. It gave promise of dynamic and thrilling adventure for this group of men, especially for the young men then in our educational institutions. It was not only to mark a new experiment in the development of body, mind, and spirit, but it would very definitely mark for all time the beginning of a new era in their Association history.

The small city of Norfolk, Virginia, was chosen as the first laboratory, but its selection was neither by chance nor choice, except from God. A year before, a small band of young colored men had felt the need of spiritual comradeship and had united for prayer and meditation. It seems something of a coincidence that they should have been discovered by a fine Christian man—an Englishman who had come across the ocean directly from the place of that first prayer circle started by Sir George Williams, the father of the Association movement. This Englishman, Mr. Joseph Smithson, and Mr. Henry E. Brown of the International Committee, made ready this prayer group, with others in Norfolk, for the coming of William Alphaeus Hunton, who was to conduct this first experiment and who was to go down in history as the first employed secretary of the Young Men's Christian Association for work among colored men.

Mr. Hunton was a very young man for a new and untried task and field, but he brought with him a knowledge, a courtesy, and a seriousness that commanded respect and even deference. Above all, he was deeply consecrated to a religion that yearned for expression in definite and practical application. He brought his gifts; and, if they could not be balanced by the gifts returned, he no doubt found some compensation in what was given him, for he did receive a warm welcome and rich hospitality, a frank eagerness to learn, an enthusiastic desire to serve, and an intelligent co-operation on the part of a goodly number.

However, coming from the environment of Ottawa to that of Norfolk was much like being transferred from the charm and advantages of a great university to a humble rural school. But he came with so much of courage and high purpose for his new work that, as I have learned to know, he was little conscious of the changes, least of all the physical ones. He did know spiritual isolation at times, for he met at Norfolk a group whose religion for the most part still expressed itself in an exuberance of emotion.

But Mr. Hunton was there and must make a completely realistic analysis of the field—of the men, the city itself, and, last but not least, of himself in relation to it. This done he promptly sat down and wrote urging that his resignation at Ottawa be accepted. Much later he received this reply:

Sir:

I beg to acknowledge the receipt of your letter of the 31st ultimo resigning your position as a third class clerk in this Dept. and while regretting that you should deem it necessary to take this step, such regret being enhanced by the knowledge I have had of your efficiency in the discharge of your duties while in the employ of the Dept., I beg to inform you that your resignation is accepted. I am, Sir,

Your obedient servant,
K. HANKOW JONES
Deputy Supt. General
of Indian Affairs

In all the intimate years of our life, he made no comment on the hardships and loneliness of that period. There were both, but, when questioned about it, he would laughingly reply, "It was all in the day's work." He would recount now and then some of the embarrassments that he sometimes suffered in those early days. Soon after he went to Norfolk there was an Emancipation celebration. As an honored citizen, he was placed in an open carriage with a number of ladies wearing the regalia of a fraternal organization. Just before the procession reached the main street of the city, these ladies felt the urge for food, stopped the carriage, bought cakes, and ate them as they rode, without sharing one iota of his distress. Again he told of being alone one day in a minister's home when a "new convert" entered and, to his consternation, in her zeal to impress upon him her new-found happiness, rather soundly trounced him before he could escape. He had a fund of these incidents connected with his early experiences in the South, some very ludicrous and some very strange, but he deeply loved the Association and friends at Norfolk to the end of his life and that city, in turn, always claimed him as its own.

The few small rooms over a store in Church Street, where the work was begun, soon became the center of interest for the colored young men of the city, especially that fine group of young men of the Presbyterian Mission College there. There were literary and debating societies, educational classes, and (with no apparatus worthy of the name), athletic work.

A library was secured when a book reception was arranged. A list of hundreds of books needed was sent out, and friends were asked not to write on the fly leaf but simply to put their names inside on a slip of paper, so that it might be possible to change books if there were duplicates, and thus insure the acquisition of new books. It was a success; hundreds of books were donated and, for that period, the Norfolk Association had an enviable library.

A fine choral club, of which Mr. Hunton was a member, came into being. It was noted for its excellence and was much in demand, not only in Norfolk, but over the entire Tidewater section.

But the deepest interest centered in Bible Study. Mr. Hunton would have it so. It commanded his closest personal attention. He would have help in this work only when it was competent and consecrated. He was filled with a deep longing to see a real development of practical Christianity. These Bible classes were the bedrock of all the Association activities. They extended to the "Women's Auxiliary," which was a strong and faithful arm of that early Association. I was not often at my home in Norfolk at that period, but I recall as if it were but yesterday going into one of those classes and hearing Mr. Hunton conduct a Bible study on just the one word "acknowledge," and our turning from book to book, chapter to chapter, and verse to verse in the Bible, wherever that one word was to be found. It gave us a habit of study that has been deeply helpful through the years, and I know it yielded richly for many who were members of the Norfolk Association at that time. A class for the study of the Sunday-school lesson by teachers was held and, for the first time, denominational barriers were broken down—a phenomenal thing at that period.

It would need a volume to record the strivings of Mr. Hunton in those three years he spent as Secretary at Norfolk—to record not only the failures and successes, the thwarted or frustrated desire for larger and better results; but also to record a very conscious knowledge that a notable change for the better was taking place in the lives of the men he had served. There had been real expansion and absorption of ideals.

Mr. Hunton was often by force of circumstances called upon to turn his splendid talents to the mere details of Association supervision, but it did not dull them for the larger needs. He was tremendously alive with drive and enthusiasm for any good work. He was taking these "first steps" with many obvious handicaps, but yet with the awareness of large responsibilities. He did it all with the high courage and abandon that only a pioneer or prophet could have. When he resigned at Norfolk at the end of three years to enter the service of the International Committee of the Young Men's Christian Association, he had come to a new and a growing regard for the most humble. He had broken through some strong and high barricades of secret sins and prejudice; he had absorbed new ideas and ideals and "increased in wisdom and stature and in favor with God and man."

Although Mr. Hunton gave three years to the work of the Norfolk Association, his last year was very much divided between that work and that of the entire field. In January, 1890, the colored Associations throughout the country—largely in schools—received the following communication from Oberlin, Ohio, written by

22

Mr. H. E. Brown, the International Secretary in charge of colored Association work:

> Poor health and pressing duties forbid my making the Southern tour this season.
> The International Committee has fortunately secured for this service W. A. Hunton, Secretary of the Norfolk Colored Association.
> He will write to you of the progress of our work and will probably be able to visit you ere long.
> May the Lord abundantly bless your labors of love for young men.

This was to be Mr Hunton's first visit over the country and especially over the deep South. At Norfolk he had, comparatively speaking, felt but slightly the shock of segregation and its attendant evils. Street cars and railroads in the state had not yet come to have their infamous "Jim Crow" laws. The one exception was the little dingy ferry that plied between the cities of Norfolk and Portsmouth; on this, accommodations were the same, but separate sides were used for colored and white patrons. Norfolk had been something of a test of his courage and sacrificial spirit, but he was now to realize in full the injustices to which his people in the South were subjected. It might be of interest, however, to remember that railroads in many Southern states had not yet been compelled by law to put on a "colored coach," and sleeping car accommodations were not so difficult to secure as they became later in a more oppressive period.

This first visit to the Associations of the colored schools of the country simply had the effect of deepening his previous convictions relative to the value of Association work for the men of his own race. He had quickened within him anew the resolve to devote his best energies to this field that he had so recently entered and was animated to a deeper concentration to this service. The following is an extract from a letter to Mr. Brown at that time:

> It seems to me, Mr. Brown, that some more definite and more active means should, if possible, be employed to provide men for the work among Colored young men. It is generally conceded that the Colleges are our only source of supply. The

23

men we need are certainly in our Colleges. What they need is inspiration, instruction and encouragement. One brief visit during the school term will not suffice to bring them to the consecration of their lives to a work which is wholly new to them and to the people among whom they are asked to labor. It was my *contact* with the *work and workers,* together with *the call* for workers *plainly heard,* that led me, by the help of God, to undertake this work. Is this not the case with every-one who has devoted his life to the work since its beginning? And can these means be supplied in greater fullness to the young men of our Colleges?

Nashville's three Colleges, Atlanta's three, Lincoln, Biddle, Claflin and Wilberforce Universities are, perhaps, the points at which candidates of the best material for our work may be found. In a short visit, the most likely men might be picked out, set apart, and directed in a course of study and line of work. Afterwards, at the proper time, the best available Association worker might be sent to each of the points named, or at which a class had been set apart, to spend two, three or even four weeks, as the case may require, in inspiring, instruct-ing and encouraging the candidates.

I write this to you, Mr. Brown, because you know better than any other man our needs and condition and because I know you will point out the practical and the impractical in my suggestion.

This opportunity that had been given him to see the South and to meet Association men was, in all probability a test of Mr. Hun-ton's fitness for the larger service to which he was now to be called. Very soon after his return to Norfolk, Mr. Richard C. Morse began correspondence with him relative to his acceptance of a position as a Secretary of the International Committee. Mr. Morse was the Executive Secretary of the Committee and had been much interested in securing Mr. Hunton for the Norfolk Association. Mr. Hunton's final letter on the subject to Mr. Morse, written December, 1890, is here quoted:

Mr. Richard C. Morse
New York City
Dear Friend:

Your letter of 16th instant has been carefully and prayer-fully considered. Nearly three years have passed since I left my native home to engage in Association work among the young men of my race in the South. And, although I have met with many difficulties and discouragements, not once have I had the desire to give up Y.M.C.A. work, but I have ever felt like pushing forward.

Circumstances connected with the work at Norfolk and the demands of the general work have required of me to perform the duties of general secretary of the Norfolk Association and also to devote a large proportion of the current year to the work of the International Committee. But my work this year has not been altogether satisfactory to me. My experience has been such as to make me feel that it is impractical for one man—for me at least—to do good work in both fields. And, as arrangements can be made for the carrying on of the work at Norfolk as suggested in your letter, I would, after conferring with the Executive Committee of the Norfolk Association, accept a call to the service of the International Committee.

I assure you that I appreciate to some extent at least, the importance of the work of the International Committee and the difficulties attending it. And, if I should engage in that work during the coming year, I would do so relying only upon the blessings of Almighty God and expecting also to receive from yourself and other Secretaries and members of the Committee that consideration, help and direction which has largely been the means of whatever success that has attended my efforts in the past.

The Norfolk people, white and colored, do not think of abandoning the work, although they realize their inability to sustain such a work as we hoped at first to carry on there. The meeting of the Advisory Board, held last Tuesday night, was encouraging, though the immediate results were not all that I had anticipated. Among other things accomplished, five new members were appointed. Another meeting will be called for early in January to provide for the current expenses for the ensuing year.

I believe that I shall ever be especially interested in the Norfolk Association and it will be a great pleasure to me to assist in the promotion of that work. After conferring with the executive Committee, I think that I will be able to suggest a practical arrangement for Norfolk. I expect to return there Monday evening; and, if I am to consider your proposition as a call from the Committee, I will begin to arrange for the change.

In January, 1891, William A. Hunton became the first colored secretary of the International Committee of the Young Men's Christian Associations, succeeding Mr. Henry E. Brown, who had given long years of service to colored people at a time when to do so entailed great hardship and required much courage. From his home in Oberlin, Ohio, Mr. Brown wrote Mr. Hunton:

Dear Hunton,

I congratulate you on the invitation you have accepted to the larger field. God bless you and keep you humble and faithful.

Shall always be glad to serve you in any way you may desire and shall hope to hear occasionally of your progress.

For the rest of his life, Mr. Brown remained a warm friend and wise counselor of Mr. Hunton, who was privileged to visit him several times.

CHAPTER FIVE

First Steps

1891-1898

MR. HUNTON began his work as an International Secretary
with a clear realization of the fact that life of itself
falls into no perfect pattern and that very hard work would be
required for the weaving of even a very simple pattern, embody-
ing the principles and objectives of the Young Men's Christian
Association.

From 1891 to 1898 he worked continuously with a steady sur-
veillance, a keen watchfulness, and an unabated ardor, all so
necessary in the first steps taken in any worth-while cause. Those
were the years when precedents established would count so largely
for future loss or gain. From this period until his death, I had
the privilege of a most intimate touch with him in his work,
and I know how earnestly he labored and how important it
seemed to him that no irreparable mistakes be made. A letter
at this time to Mr. Erskine Uhl, Office Secretary of the International Committee, illustrates this point:

> I think that quiet meetings of workers from a few Associa-
> tions, such as was held at Nashville last spring, would be de-
> cidedly helpful to our work. We could call such a meeting
> to be held in Richmond some time in March, with the hope
> of having representatives from six or eight college and local
> Associations.
>
> In the tour which I am about to make I might be able to
> arrange for the holding during the coming fall of similar meet-
> ings at convenient points in North Carolina, South Carolina,
> Georgia and Kentucky.

The opening of the Association at Norfolk had given strong
impetus to the desire for organization in a number of cities and,
in a few, the urge to organize at all costs. One of the most inter-

esting experiments of that period, and perhaps interesting to the Harlem of today, was the effort as early as 1890 to organize a branch of the Association in that section of New York. After spending some time with the group in Harlem, Mr. Hunton sent his report to Mr. Richard McBurney, who was then the General Secretary of the New York City Association. It reads:

Dear Sir:

There is an effort being made by colored men to establish a Young Men's Christian Association in Harlem. I have met the pastors of the churches, a few colored business men of that community, and also many of the young men connected with the movement.

I have learned that the colored people in Harlem have but recently gone there from other parts of the city and that their institutions, including their four churches, are yet in the early stages of development. But few of the best families of the colored people of the city live in Harlem and none of the old and flourishing churches are in that locality.

Yet there is there a large population of colored people, of the laboring class, and it may well be considered as being one of the three sections of this great city needing Association work among their young men. One hundredth Street and Third Avenue may perhaps be considered the center of this section.

The Association, already organized and known as Branch Number Two of Harlem, is managed by an Executive Board of seven members, four of whom are the pastors of the four churches already referred to. The direction and promotion of the movement so far has been almost wholly in the hands of these Ministers, with the Reverend J. R. R. Smith as leader.

The Association has a membership of about seventy-five, nearly all of whom, I am told, are reliable young men. I met thirty of these young men on Sunday afternoon and spoke to them of the greatness and importance of the work they desired to undertake, of some of the difficulties to be overcome and of the personal sacrifice that is necessary to be made in order to secure success and asked them if they were *quite sure* that they are prepared to go forward. They, all as one man, expressed themselves as being sincere and as being willing and determined to do their best to make the effort successful.

In a conference this morning with a few of the leaders of the movement in question, careful consideration was given to the probable cost of the work and to the means of support.

28

It was thought that about three hundred and fifty dollars could be raised by the colored people for the first year's work, while the cost of the work for the first year, including furniture, would be from six hundred and fifty dollars to one thousand dollars—the difference depending upon the amount to be paid for the services of a secretary, which would depend upon his qualifications and upon the proportion of time he would devote to the work of the Association.

The members of this Association desire that it shall be a Branch of the Young Men's Christian Association of the city and are willing to adopt such means as are necessary to secure that relation. And now I beg to state:

(1) That, while the colored people of either of the other two sections referred to of this city have among them better material for Association work and have arrived at a stage of development more favorable, perhaps, for the supporting and promotion of that work, I think the people of Harlem are ready to give the matter a fair and earnest trial and, if they are well supported, there are hopeful prospects of success.

(2) That the proposed Association should be a Branch of the New York City Association.

(3) That, if undertaken at all, the work should be genuine, and the services of a good secretary should be secured. The fact that the people are comparatively ignorant as to the scope of methods of Association work, increases the need of the services and full time of a qualified secretary.

Trusting that this report of my investigations will enable you to take proper action in regard to the matter herein referred to, I remain.

This effort seems to have failed of recognition, but an Association was soon organized in Fifty-third Street, which was then the center of Negro life in New York City. The Rev. C. T. Walker, an esteemed Baptist minister of that day, stood at the forefront of the organization and had the help of Mr. Thomas Bell as an earnest and faithful Secretary. That was the beginning of what is now the One Hundred and Thirty-fifth Street Branch.

By 1892 Mr. Hunton was not only supervising student work, holding conferences, as suggested to Mr. Uhl, and frequently meeting the International Staff in New York and at other points, but he was trying to study methods and principles for working with a handicapped group and organizing and *dis-organizing* city Associations. The latter seems to have been as an important work in those early days as the former. He wrote from a certain city:

It may be that I am a better dis-organizer than organizer, for I have broken up an Association here three times. It was necessary, and now I think we will have a good start.

The organization of city Associations at Washington and Louisville claimed much of his time in the first years of his labors, and the advancement of the Norfolk Association was very close to his heart. But it was not until January, 1892, that he could write about Norfolk:

Perhaps I had better tell you first that it is done. The lot on Queen Street, formerly owned by Reverend Spiller, now belongs to the Young Men's Christian Association. The deed was executed December thirtieth, and the cash was paid yesterday. No one feels more relieved than I do. But I will tell you more about my recent experiences in that connection when my time is not so limited.

Writing from Norfolk again in April of that same year he said:

You will be glad to know that work here is really growing. We are going to have here one of the best Associations among colored men.

April 20, 1892, was a memorable date. It marked the time of his first meeting with Mr. J. E. Moorland, who, at a later period, was to become his associate. Writing from Washington, he remarked:

You will be glad to know that our work here is progressing nicely. I think Washington is going to have the very best Association among colored men. Their Secretary, a Mr. J. E. Moorland, arrived yesterday and is with me as I am writing to you. I never saw him before yesterday, but I rather like him already.

Late in 1892 came this cheering word from Louisville, Kentucky:

We have raised six hundred dollars of the one thousand needed for the first year's work, and now I am going to certain men in Oberlin and other cities to secure the four hundred still needed.

Seeing the need of some check and guidance being put upon the eagerness to organize, Mr. Hunton wrote his first Association pamphlet in 1892, giving it the title *First Steps*. This simple and brief pamphlet answered the need for governing the organization of colored Associations, and was used very generally by all the International Staff and State Secretaries, having had several reprints. With the omission of the recommended readings, we give here the essential parts of the pamphlet.

The history of the Young Men's Christian Association has been, in the main, very encouraging. The growth of the work during the past fifteen years has been marvelous, as shown in the accumulation of property, in the erection and equipment of magnificent buildings, and in the development of the religious, intellectual, and physical departments of the work. But while prosperity and success have attended Association work in many communities, in others such sad and damaging failure has been experienced that, on reviewing the whole, it seems wise and necessary to sound a few notes of warning for the help of those who are contemplating the organization of new Associations. For they need to know that there are hazardous methods which lead to certain and sudden disaster.

There are now—April 1, 1892—1,424 Young Men's Christian Associations in North America. But if all the Associations that have ever been organized were in existence today, there would be at least three times that number. During each succeeding year, many new Associations have indeed been added to the list in the Year Book, but many others, in the meantime have "died," and have been "dropped" from the list. Almost every State and Provincial Convention, while rejoicing over the new and promising Associations organized during the year, is called upon also to sadly mourn the death of not a few.

There are, doubtless, many causes which lead to the untimely death of Associations, all of which might with much profit be considered. But it is the object of this paper to call attention to one very general cause of the sickly life and untimely death of a very large portion, if not a majority, of the Associations which have been dropped; and in so doing we shall endeavor also to answer the oft-repeated question—"What steps should be taken to organize a Young Men's Christian Association?"

In almost every community there are some young men who, on hearing of the progress of the work and of the advantages which it brings, are moved with a desire to organize an Association. Such young men desire a good thing, and they should seek and receive encouragement and assistance from those who are able to help them. But they too frequently adopt such a hasty plan of action as to utterly defeat the worthy object they have in view. A mass meeting is called, the marvelous results accomplished in other places by Associations are painted in glowing colors, their desire to organize an Association is strongly expressed and enthusiastically endorsed, and resolutions are adopted setting forth the "peculiar" needs of their "peculiar" place, and urging the State or International Committee to send a secretary "at once" to organize an Association while things are "booming."

It has been customary, in answer to such appeals, to recommend a weekly meeting of men only, for prayer and Bible study, and for the consideration of the principles and methods of Young Men's Christian Association work; and to advise that such meetings be continued regularly through six or twelve months, or for such a time as may be needed to prepare the way for the inauguration of the work. But this process has been considered too slow by many. Hence, in the hasty way already referred to, another meeting is called; a constitution is secured; an organization is effected; and they plunge headlong into the work, into debt, and into a multitude of troubles, which result in the unhappy death of the movement.

Thus the dry bones of dead Associations lie bleaching in the sun all along the way from Dan to Beersheba. Much zeal and enthusiasm have been wasted, and business men have become impatient with the failure of such misguided efforts. It is needless to add that it were far better if such Associations had never been organized.

Such hasty efforts, then, are the great evil against which we raise a warning voice. If a man were about to engage in the grocery business for the first time, he would take time to carefully consider its peculiar nature, its relation to other lines of business, how much capital he would have to invest, and whether he could raise the amount needed or not; and he would also study the experience of other men in the same line of business, that he might be able to avoid their mistakes and also might know a bargain when he saw one. Would we not expect men who are about to engage in a special line of Christian work to exercise as much care and good judgment as if they were about to engage in some secular pursuit?

If you want to organize a Young Men's Christian Association, "make haste *slowly.*" Look well into the matter. The following suggestions are based upon experience:

1. Express your desire to organize an Association to the *Christian young men* of your community, one at a time, and urge the matter upon their attention, earnestly and prayerfully, until at least ten or a dozen share your desire and are willing to co-operate.

2. From these earnest Christian fellows and others like them who may be added to your ranks from time to time form a "Young Men's Band" and appoint a time for a weekly meeting for prayer and the consideration of the work you desire to undertake. No constitution is needed at present. These meetings should be held promptly and regularly at the home of one of the members of the band. No meeting should, as a rule, be longer than an hour and a half. Much of this time should be spent in offering short, earnest prayers.

3. Appoint a competent leader and a faithful secretary of the band, and take up the short course of study outlined below. This course includes ten important lessons. With one lesson each week, the work of "getting ready to organize" may be completed in a little more than two months, during which time the half-hearted volunteers will drop out, leaving a few intelligent and determined Christian workers as excellent material for a good foundation. This is not losing time by any means. The half-hearted fellows will fall in later as they see the work advancing.

Having finished the course of study, and being sure that the first two conditions laid down in "Lesson 2" are satisfied, your next step will be to write to the State or International Committee, stating how long your band has been organized, the number of members at the beginning and the number at the end of the study, and whether you think the time is ripe for the commencement of the work; and requesting the Committee to send one of its secretaries to direct and assist you in making further investigations regarding the organization of an Association.

In the pamphlet quoted, one readily senses some of the difficulties involved in organizing an Association during that early period. Writing from a North Carolina town along this line, Mr. Hunton said:

I did not get to bed until after one o'clock last night. You ask why I was up so late? Well, I was giving some men "Hail Columbia." I really was. They have what they call a Young Men's Christian Association and are attracting considerable attention in the city but they have not the first elements of a successful work. I tell you I went for them and they took it well. But nothing less would have aroused them. I did it kindly, pouring oil on the wounds that I had purposely made. After all it was a real good meeting!

Certainly this early work of supervision of both student and city Associations, especially the latter, required an unusual astuteness and with it an infinite patience. There were not only the problems of the organizations themselves to be solved but also those of their relation to the whole field of Association activity. Again and again Mr. Hunton found it necessary to express his own ideas on guiding principles in these relationships, which were, for the most part, so utterly in contrast with his own background of experience. He very early wrote, while in New York City, as follows:

> After thorough investigation I do not find one Young Men's Christian Association, either in Brooklyn, Boston, New York, Chicago, and most other Northern cities, that has as many as one dozen colored young men in its membership. This is a startling fact, and it seems to me it should lead us to vigorous effort in reaching these men.
> The colored clergymen of Brooklyn have made application for a branch, to be managed by colored men, having a colored secretary and doing work among colored men. And there has been conducted in the Central Association Building in this city a Bible class of colored men, looking forward to the establishment of such a department among them. It seems very clear to me that the time must come, and that very soon, when our Associations shall stretch out a strong hand that these men may be helped, and that influences, such as are benefitting white young men of the country, may also be used on behalf of colored young men.
> When we turn to the South the picture is more gloomy. Not only do the local Associations not reach the colored men, but we find also that the State Committees do not reach out to the colored men, so that whatever of supervision and extension is done in the South on behalf of colored men has been done and must be done through the International Committee alone. For many years we have carried on this work chiefly in the schools and colleges, but more recently it has been organ-

ized in a few of the larger cities and towns, and the Committee is urgently petitioned to extend the work more rapidly than its present force and resources will allow.

He was often approached on this matter by secretaries of the other group. In the North, it was the question of the admission of colored men to their Associations. Mr. Hunton was always both frank and positive in his convictions. But with his candor there was always the saving grace of tactfulness and innate culture that precluded the possibility of offensiveness. A secretary in a western state, who found himself in great difficulty on this point, wrote him, and a copy of Mr. Hunton's reply is here given:

My dear Brother:
  Your letter of September 26 was duly received at Richmond, Virginia, but I delayed my reply in order to give the subject referred to the consideration its importance deserves.
  It is understood that one of the main principles on which Y.M.C.A. work is based is that expressed in the membership clause of the constitution—which provides that *any* young man satisfying certain conditions may become a member.
  All admit that the spirit of our work demands that this part of our constitution be strictly observed; and that all young men satisfying the conditions laid down should be admitted to membership.
  Yet, I regret to say, there are three different ways of treating colored applicants by white Associations in the United States, according to the existence of much or but little race prejudice in the respective communities—as follows:
  1. In the South, where race prejudice is very strong, the white Associations proclaim, without any uncertainty, that they do not want and will not receive colored men as members. The result is they never gain an appreciation of the colored man.
  2. Throughout the Middle States and occasionally in a Northern State, the white Associations "pigeon-hole" applications from colored men. Sometimes the colored applicant does not push the matter and nothing more is heard of it. But more frequently such trouble is experienced as that from which you are now suffering, and the work is often seriously hindered.
  3. The third method of treatment, and, I believe, the only one endorsed by the International Committee, is that which accords to colored applicants the very same treatment given to

white. If they satisfy the conditions of membership they are so informed. I know of several white Associations in the North with from one to a dozen colored members; seldom, if ever, more than a dozen, and they are usually of the best element among colored young men; for colored men do not join white Associations in large numbers even under most favorable circumstances.

These Associations have experienced no serious trouble. A few white men sometimes protest against the presence of the colored member. But when the Secretary, backed by the Board of Directors, brings them face to face with the constitution and the moral issue at stake, and gives them to understand that ours is a brotherhood and that there can be no compromise of principle, the objectors yield and usually remain in the Association too.

The second method referred to above is evidently weak and unwise, and it almost always causes trouble. And whether the first or third method stated should be adopted by an Association must depend upon local conditions.

I hope your city is not quite so bad as you seem to think it is. Often opposition against the colored man is started by but a few individuals, and those in authority yield to the unreasonable demands of the few without any effort to bring their better judgment to bear against them. Peace and prosperity are assured to those who dare to do as our Lord would do were He in the flesh among the men of the United States today.

With brotherly affection and in all frankness.

In 1893 he wrote Mr. Morse about the city Associations in the South as follows:

The more I study the difficulties with which we meet in our work in the South and the causes which painfully retard the progress of that work, the stronger the conviction grows upon me that the work among the colored young men of that section needs financial assistance other than what can be secured locally. But how to provide this needed assistance and how best to administer it are not easily determined. However, I submit the following for the consideration of the Committee.

1. Whatever outside assistance is administered, it should be secured by or through the International Committee. For the Committee to undertake to endorse the agents of local Associations who might be sent out to solicit aid would not only open the way for the flooding of the country with such

36

agents but also make it possible and comparatively easy for impostors to undermine our work.

There are two sources open to the Committee from which funds may be secured for ·this advance work.

2. The Colored Associations already in existence. A glance at the Year Book shows that in 1891, nine colored Associations gave only twenty-three dollars and seventy-nine cents toward the work of the International Committee. Now the importance and necessity of general and more liberal contributions being made toward the funds of the Committee by the thirty-six colored Associations has never been pressed, except in one or two cases. If these plans are approved I have reason to believe that we will be able to secure from all our Associations an average contribution of about twenty dollars each, college and local, per year.

3. The other and, we trust, more fruitful source is from our friends in the Northern States and in Canada. In some instances it may be possible to present the claims of this special department of the work before State and Provincial Conventions with a view to securing special aid. Correspondence with State Committees prior to the meeting of conventions would determine when this would be practicable and when not.

Again, parlor conferences or mass meetings might be arranged for by prosperous local Associations in Northern and Canadian cities at which the claims of the work referred to might be strongly presented and assistance secured. The meetings, lastly, might be followed up by personal appeals such as may be suggested by local bands of Secretaries.

It was in the summer of 1893, in that very important period when he was so earnestly making an effort for a true and firm foundation for Association work among colored men, that Mr. Hunton and I were married at my home in Norfolk, Virginia. And to him, in a sense, it was home too, for he was still giving all the time possible to Association work there and also using it as a base for his Southern work.

Although I was not in Norfolk very much at this very early period of Mr. Hunton's activities, I had met him and had some little association with him. However, in the summer of 1890, hearing that I was going to Wilberforce University to visit my sister, he said to my father, who had become one of his good supporters, that he would be on his way to his home in Canada and would be very glad to accompany me as far as Cincinnati and put me on the right train to Xenia. As girls very rarely traveled alone at that time, my father was pleased to accept his offer, and thus began the friendship that resulted in our marriage.

I had been at school in the North and then had taught in another city, and was teaching in Alabama just before our marriage, so that our courtship proceeded for the most part by correspondence—a very close and revealing one that led me to know how he fared in various places and that has enabled me to write about his work with so much surety.

I had not the slightest doubt of my love for Mr. Hunton, but there was, I confess, some mingling of awe in my attitude toward him at first. For he was so different from the average young man in his general manners and earnestness of purpose that my girl friends used to say that I might see him depart much in the way that Elijah disappeared from the earth. He was an unusually high-minded person, but, even before we were married I learned to know that he was also a very human person. He needed and wanted love and affection.

He knew how to relax from the concerns of his work and enjoy hearty fun. Once he took me to see a "Wild West Show" in which Buffalo Bill was the main attraction. Great was my surprise and gone was my feeling of awe when Mr. Hunton yelled, whistled, clapped his knees, and waved his hat with the abandon of all the other "fans" there. He would recover just long enough to apologize for his over-exuberance and then go off again. I enjoyed him much more than I did the entertainment though, of course, I did not tell him that, and I felt well paid for that experience in my discovery that the belief of my girl friends was but a fallacy.

Moreover, as I have re-read his letters, I have been surprised at the frequency with which he referred to his food—good, bad or indifferent—as he traveled about, this despite the fact that he was a very moderate eater. Once he had written:

> I wish you would send me a little home-made wheat by telephone. Coarse corn-meal with a little salt and water added and then cooked is a favorite dish down this way. Shall I bring you a sample in my pocket? But I forget that you

38

live in Virginia and must be familiar with the Virginia hoe-cake.

The three years before our marriage, when we wrote to each other almost daily, was a period long enough for me to learn just how Mr. Hunton and I would be separated oftener than otherwise after our married life came and, although we were very close in spirit, that my contentment depended upon finding some satisfying compensation for this physical separation. Mr. Hunton had written me from Northfield in 1891:

> I want to know my Lord so well that in all circumstances I can say it is well. I am sure that you will understand me, dear, when I say that I have decided to make everything subservient to the best interests of the work that the Lord has committed to me.

Before I could go to the altar I had to find my answer and, though I was extremely young and extremely inexperienced, it came to me that my way out would be in making his life mine. This not only proved true, but it had the added value of leading me into new avenues of satisfying usefulness. For more than a decade I did most of Mr. Hunton's secretarial work and went with him to conferences when possible, looking after details and advising and inspiring him. I edited the little sheet known as the *Messenger*, although D. Webster Davis was the known editor. But from it all I gained far more than I gave. Being so close to him in his work for so long a period was the thing that gave me the opportunity to earn the name of pioneer in the organization of women so closely related to the Young Men's Christian Association.

Working with my husband, I learned a great deal about the source of his strength that enabled him to persevere in the face of great difficulties. He had the habit of serenity that could not be easily disturbed. It was his by virtue of inheritance, but it had been greatly deepened through those processes that led to his early consecration. He also had a faith to the end of his life that reality, however crude or even cruel, could by patient effort be somehow lifted to the realm of idealism; he had the faculty of making other men feel this faith of his. He was always conservative in

39

opinion and expression and never dogmatic. He spurned narrowness and pettiness. He had a deep appreciation of his fellows and a willingness to learn all that would be helpful to him. But he avoided the vain controversies and appeals of self-interested people. Holding to his own ideals in the midst of confusion, he earnestly endeavored to lead men to see clearly and live honestly.

The year 1894 was one of the most memorable and important in Mr. Hunton's whole life. He was chosen as one of the American delegation to the Golden Jubilee of the Young Men's Christian Association, which was held in London that year. The colored Associations, under the leadership of Dr. R. R. Moton, then Commandant at Hampton Institute, and always a most enthusiastic Association leader, took great pride in partly financing that trip, and thus showing to the International Committee their appreciation of Mr. Hunton's service. With other members of the International staff, he was the guest of Mr. James Stokes in Paris immediately after the London Convention. His first address relative to this event after his return was made before the students of Hampton Institute and was printed in the *Southern Workman.* It is given later in this volume.

The next four years witnessed something of recognition and reward for earnest pioneer efforts that he had hardly anticipated would come so soon.

Early in 1896 he wrote very jubilantly as follows:

A change has been made at New York that I like very much. I do not know that I spoke to you about it, but I have not been satisfied with the little attention given my work by the Committee. I have been making my own plans and programs and carrying them out with but little, if any, criticism from the Committee. Of late I have felt this responsibility too much and was about to write Mr. Morse accordingly. I received a letter Saturday, stating that the Chairman had requested Mr. Cephas Brainerd, Junior, to take a special relation to my work and he has written for such information as shows that he desires to become intelligent on the subject. He approved my last program and says he thinks I should go to Wilberforce. He asks for a catalogue of that school and of some others that I am now visiting. That is business and will be a source of inspiration to me. I know Mr. Brainerd and am glad he is the man with whom I am to work in such a relation. I hope to have him blowing my horn for me.

This was the beginning of what developed into a Special Committee from the International Committee, for direct relation with the Colored Men's Department. Colored men, especially religious and educational leaders, had begun to grasp the significance and value of Association work and to give it more sympathy and help. After one of Mr. Hunton's annual visits to Tuskegee at this period, Mr. Booker T. Washington expressed himself thus:

> My Dear Sir:
>
> I regret very much that I was not able to be at Tuskegee upon the occasion of your recent visit there. I am advised that in every way your presence was an inspiration to our students. I want to thank you again for the visit. I have written Mr. Morse and now beg to advise you that I shall be glad to serve you in an advisory capacity whenever possible.
>
> I trust you find much of encouragement and hope as you go among the people of our race.

Writing from Columbia, South Carolina, Mr. Hunton exclaimed:

> The Lord gave us a glorious day yesterday! I made four addresses, two in churches, one at the Young Men's Christian Association and one at Benedict College. I had great liberty of speech at all, and a splendid impression has been made in favor of the work. I made an address at Allen this morning and also at the Ministers' Union. Several ministers who have been indifferent or opposed have been won over. The Lord has used us mightily here, and I give him praise.

In 1896 Mr. Hunton made the following report:

82 Associations in Colored institutions are in existence.
10 have been organized this year.
77 report 11,276 young men students in their institutions.
62 report 6,077 young men, students in their institutions, members of evangelical churches.
74 report a total membership of 5,064.
74 report an active membership of 3,987.
64 report 1,268 men serving on committees.
35 report 2,097 young men's meetings, with a total attendance of 89,664.

49 report 1,352 Bible class sessions with a total attendance of 17,916.
28 report 189 missionary meetings.
52 report 286 lectures.
37 report 94 socials.
40 report Association rooms.
24 report 1,363 volumes in libraries.
40 observed the week of prayer in November.
41 observed the day of prayer in February.
11 report 56 volunteers.
 9 report 302 men in mission study.
10 report $112 given to missions.
21 report subscribers for the INTERCOLLEGIAN.
 2 conducted fall campaigns.
44 reported 358 conversions.
24 report 115 of the men converted united with churches.
15 report furniture valued at $1,049.
21 report $103 given to the International Committee.
 8 report $42 given to the State Committee.

This, in bare statistics, was the total of the results of those "first steps" for the salvation of a group of men—not yet all free from the traditions and customs of a long era of bondage nor yet, in most places, full citizens—but these first steps had been made with a united and blessed faith that knew no surrender. They opened a trail for that larger recognition and reward and for the magnificent achievements that, though then unseen, were just ahead.

These statistics could in no sense give a conception of the tasks of almost inconceivable scope—difficult and even overwhelming in their attendant problems—that had to be successfully performed before the stable and effective organization of Association work among colored men could be attained.

At this time Mr. Hunton, out of ten years of experience, wrote with a high and courageous conviction:

An entrance into this extensive field of labor has been made. We confidently expect that this work will be thoroughly established among colored young men throughout the United States, and will eventually become a mighty factor in the evangelization of the young man of Africa.

One of the happy experiences of this period was his return to

Ottawa in 1898—just ten years after he had left to enter Young Men's Christian Association work. There was unbounded joy not only on his part but among his Ottawa friends. They gave him a triumphal entry because he had conquered the unknown and returned as their brave warrior. He had endured hardship as a good soldier of Jesus Christ: he had found companionship in marriage and the very human joy of fatherhood and had steadily advanced in the work to which he had been called and which had become of supreme importance to him.

Writing on the night of his arrival there in April, 1898, he gave expression to his happiness thus:

> I cannot refrain from writing to you tonight, if only to say— I am here in Ottawa. It is like a dream. I know of no place that I would rather live than in this city, all other things being equal (whatever that phrase means). I left N. Y. at 6:25 last night and arrived here at 11:20 this A. M. To my surprise the Secretaries, Mr. Fedarb and Mr. Gilbert were at the depot to meet me. My! How I have been going since. Am stopping with Mr. Campbell, one of my dear old chums. He married since I left and has two little girls. Have been over to the Department of Indian Affairs and had a good time with my former associates in the office. Some have died and some show evident signs of age. Have seen lots of other friends.
>
> A strange coincidence this morning. Mr. Fedarb and I went into the House of Commons and were there only a minute or two when the member from Chatham arose and spoke in explanation of some charges that had been made against the government for discharging colored men employed on the Government Railroad. All that was said was highly commendable to the colored men, and the charges against the Government were denied. I presume that a talk about the colored people as a class is not heard in Parliament once in two or three years. Sweetheart, I wish you were here to see how different these people are from many white people we know. I wish you were here to enjoy these days with me. But I must close and go to bed, for I shall have heavy work here, whether I get any money or not.

His enthusiasm during this visit continued to effervesce in his letters to me. He writes:

> On entering the Association building this A. M. there was a large bulletin board, with a large photo of me hung in the

center, announcing a reception in my honor for tonight. There is to be a "Drawing Room" tomorrow at 4 to which you are invited. I address the Boy's Meeting Friday night, the Men's Meeting Saturday night, and speak in two of the largest churches Sunday. There may be another "Drawing Room" Monday. I could write you all day about this city and the people, but I must get at some other work.

And still again:

The "Drawing Room" was held at Mrs. Blackburn's. She gave $50 for the work and $10 for my personal use. The old and new members of the Junior Department gave me a handsome Bible-Bagster, levant, silk-sewed, and interleaved. I am very proud of it, you may be sure.

You remember my friend Mr. Judkin who came to Norfolk to see me when I was living with Mrs. Cook. I am to take tea with him this evening. And Mr. Kuhling who was Secretary of the Y.M.C.A. when I was at Ottawa is now pastor of an Episcopal Church here and I am to dine with him today. I expected to speak once yesterday, but spoke three times. McGill University, the City Association and the Congregational Church.

The reception was very pleasant indeed. I met many old friends, both ladies and gentlemen, as well as many young people who have grown up from boyhood and girlhood. Some of the clerks from the Indian Department were out and it was a very happy time for me. This is one of the few places on this continent, perhaps the only one where I feel perfectly free anywhere I go.

Always, Ottawa remained for him an ideal in human relationships which he could vision in days when the reality about him was in such strong contrast. He was deeply grateful for his experience there—an experience which helped to hold his faith in trying times. A visit to Ottawa together was one of the unfulfilled dreams of our united life.

It was in 1898 that the Spanish American war cloud began to dim the horizon and absorb public interest. Mr. Hunton at that time was on his very happy visit to Ottawa and wrote rather jocularly in March about getting our boy—a mere baby—prepared for the fray. But in a day or two afterward he wrote again in serious mood:

44

I see that the colored soldiers have been ordered to Dry Tortugas, but let us think of peace rather than war. There is so much work to be done.

Later in the month, after his return to the States, he wrote as follows:

The war cloud is lowering and wealthy and timid people are afraid. But I still think that a clash will be avoided, although I may be mistaken. Times will be very hard if there is a fight of even short duration.

In April he was in Boston and commented as follows:

Nearer and nearer the Spanish-American crisis is approaching. The money kings or arbitration must now be relied upon to avert active hostilities. It is all the talk up this way.

Then a ray of light:

There is a rift in the clouds today. McKinley may honorably avert war. I hope so. A few days will decide it.

Thus far there had been no awareness in Mr. Hunton's mind, apparently, that he was to enter in any way into this war preparation, but he was set to work almost immediately, and, though regretting the necessity for it, he became enthusiastic about the Young Men's Christian Association activities in the camps.

As early as June 6, 1898, he wrote:

Five members of my Army Committee will be organized this P. M. We have sent letters to 15 others who will be members. Printed circulars will be out tomorrow; have nearly secured a tent which we expect to have up at Fort Macon by Saturday in charge of Prof. Bruce. I will then go to Chickamauga or Tampa.

The same month he wrote from Washington:

I stopped here to inquire into work at Camp Alger and find it necessary to go out to the camp nine miles with International Secretary Moore. Mr. Prince A. Goines is in charge of the Y.M.C.A. tent for Major Young's command and Moore wants me to see how the work prospers.

The next day, June 30, he described the work at this camp:

Well, I spent several hours at Camp Alger, nine miles from

45

Washington where there are twenty thousand troops. The Committee has twelve Young Men's Christian Association tents in the camp. Tent number two is near Major Young's battalion and in charge of Mr. Goines. The secretaries provide their own board, or rather have it provided in their own dining tent. I had supper with them last night. I saw about 6,000 troops on parade last night and about the camp all was hustle and bustle. Major Young has three companies in his command. He hopes to increase it to six companies and then he will be made a colonel of a regiment.

Both this Major and the Major of the North Carolina Colored troops at Fort Macon are named Young. Let us not get them mixed.

At Fort Macon there were three companies of two hundred and forty men, making a battalion. By the end of this week they expect to have a regiment of eight hundred to one thousand men and Young will be a colonel.

I was highly pleased with the bearing of the officers and men at Fort Macon. The discipline was very good and the men seemed to be proud of having colored officers. Everything worked smoothly. There are a lot of tough characters in each company, but they are kept under subjection.

He had little time for the promotion of his regular work, for he not only had to organize camp work and find men to supervise it, but also raise funds to help support it. From Richmond in July he wrote:

Have been canvassing today for the Camp work. We have a fine tent at "Camp Corbin," ten miles from here on the C. & O. There are five hundred and forty men there from Richmond, Petersburg, Lynchburg, Danville, etc. There is another company to come from Petersburg and two from Norfolk.

He was in Macon, Georgia, in November of that year when the colored soldiers from Virginia had real trouble there. His comment was:

The Virginia regiment is in disgrace, the whole lot being under arrest. Poor Mr. Blue says it is his first experience to be under arrest. He was searched with the rest.

When they came to Macon, and before they were put under strict discipline, many of them secured whiskey. The first night here, they went to a park and cut down a tree on which a colored youth had been lynched some years ago. Some

46

guards tried to arrest them, they resisted and were finally put under arrest.

They have been strictly guarded for ten days. Not a man is allowed across the line without a pass, nor to enter without a pass. I could not get in today, but hope to succeed tomorrow.

Finally he wrote:

All Colored troops now in America, except Twenty-Fourth and Twenty-Fifth Regular Infantry and Ninth Regular Cavalry, are to be stationed in winter quarters in South with white regiments, usually two white and one colored regiment forming a brigade. There will be seven colored regiments in these winter quarters held ready for service in Porto Rico or Cuba when needed. Four in Macon, Georgia; two Ohio battalions in Summerville, South Carolina, and the Alabama Regiment and Tenth Cavalry in Anniston, Alabama.

I have recommended that we have six tents with these troops in their winter quarters, etc. They move about November first.

This war experience increased rather than diminished Mr. Hunton's belief in peace, and at the same time it taught him a new value of his work—its power to maintain the high morale of men in unique situations and to make many of them spiritually strong in the midst of opposing forces. He realized anew and more clearly the assured stability of Association work. It gave to him, moreover, the opportunity to meet many fine men and to have close contact with them. His war executive committee had been built up of colored men of high repute, with the Honorable E. A. Johnson, then of Raleigh, North Carolina, as Chairman. Men from among the war secretaries were drawn permanently into Association work. I think especially of Mr. Rufus Meroney, a Texan and a Yale man, whom Mr. Hunton first met in a Texas camp and who was utterly won for Association work. His name is still revered in Brooklyn, where as secretary he devoted his whole splendid life to the movement.

Mr. Hunton was very happy when the war was over and he could turn his thoughts to the regular stream of Association activity, for there were new and important developments to take place.

CHAPTER SIX

Widening Horizons

1898-1911

A T T H E beginning of 1898, Mr. Hunton was very seriously concerned about the future of this movement among colored men to which he had devoted the past ten years. Although he experienced a certain sense of satisfaction for what had been accomplished and was sure of the approval and support of the International Committee, he realized that what had been done might have been better done, and that the cold light of criticism should be thrown upon his field before he made new steps in any direction. He could clearly distinguish some underlying issues that must be faced eventually, and had an awareness even then that the flood-time of success might bring with it unseen and unknown obstacles to dam the stream. Although his war activities and regular Association work had kept him afield for the most part, he had given much time to deep devotions, seeking a re-consecration and a new vitalizing force to meet the future.

Since 1895, he had been feeling more and more convinced that the time was rapidly drawing near when he must have help, in order to be better prepared to meet the larger opportunities and more arduous responsibilities that he could vision ahead. Moreover, he needed an added strength to hold the advantages he had already gained.

With reference to his multiplying responsibilities and the relative importance of student work at this period, he wrote Mr. Richard C. Morse the following letter:

> I received your letter of the 23rd instant, in which you refer to the statement of the newly elected chairman of the International Committee, Dr. L. C. Warner, to the effect that the principal emphasis of the work of the committee in the Colored

Men's Department, through its secretary, should be given to the College Associations, etc.

In reply I would say that while it is evident that more time should be given for the supervision and development of the college work, I do not think the best interests of my department would be served by devoting any less time and energy to the city Associations than is now given.

I have noted with much uneasiness and dissatisfaction year by year that I have had to respond more and more frequently to calls from City Associations at the expense of a proper supervision and needed extension of my college field. I have yielded very unwillingly to this steadily increasing demand, for, I have found the college work more delightful than the local and, as Dr. Warner says, it yields more remunerative results from the amount of effort put forth. But for the reasons and considerations, I herewith submit, I have considered that course essential to the proper growth of the college work as well as of the department as a whole.

1. The share that college graduates will take in city Association work will depend not only upon the degree of interest they develop as students but also upon their finding some Association work to do in the cities when their college careers are completed. Otherwise they become absorbed in other lines of activity and will, afterward, be almost as difficult to enlist in our work as men who had never been members of a college association. I do not mean, of course, that the good influence of college is lost upon such men. Far from it! But that the probability of them not being of service to the Association movement after college life increases immensely if they find no city avenue in which to gratify their love for the work and develop their talent.

2. It is a powerful stimulant to the college movement to show possibilities of Association work in cities. I believe it is true that we never had a well organized and aggressive college organization until after something practical and tangible was done at Norfolk and Richmond, and it is certain that the college associations of Virginia are better organized and more fruitful than those of any other state—partly because, I believe, we have fine city Associations in that state with which many of the students have been brought into touch.

3. Our present possessions may be enlarged to my vision beyond their real value. Yet it seems to me that to hold and develop what we have already of fruitful and hopeful city associations—to say nothing about the organization of new work, which it has been impossible to prevent, will require even more

49

time of a supervising agent than has as yet been given. Baltimore, Washington, Richmond and Norfolk are local points that must be held and developed, and at no small expenditure of time of the secretary of the Committee. While the organizations at New Haven, Connecticut, Camden, New Jersey, Louisville, Kentucky, Wilmington, North Carolina, Lynchburg and Petersburg, Virginia, should be encouraged and directed by personal visitation. There are at least eight other organized local points of comparative minor importance.

The above is stated without any reference to the recognized and absolute need of something being done in the line of our work among the thousands of colored young men in our larger cities.

I confess that I do not see how I am to meet the demands that are now made upon my time. Perhaps the best policy to pursue is to develop the city organizations first mentioned above and then to give the decided preference to college work.

And now, both in his reports to and interviews with the International Committee, he began stressing the urgency of this need. Meantime, he was making an earnest effort to convince Mr. J. E. Moorland that an important and extensive field had deep need for his service. Writing to me from New Haven early in 1898, he said:

I am thinking of urging Mr. Moorland to come into the service of the International Committee. We must have someone with experience. His experience at Washington was very valuable. His work at Nashville and Cleveland has been most successful. He is the man, I think. What do you think?

From the time in 1892 when Mr. Moorland had first entered the work of the Young Men's Christian Association at Washington, D. C., and on through the years, the relation between him and Mr. Hunton had been very warm and helpful. Although Mr. Moorland did not continue in the work very long at that period, he continued to give it his full sympathy and support and to render very valuable aid in the many city and student conferences held in those years. The bond of friendship between these two men gradually grew stronger and closer. During his visits to Nashville, when Mr. Moorland was in the ministry there, Mr. Hunton always wrote with joy and affection of Mr. and Mrs. Moorland,

and the same was true when later they went to Cleveland. Again and again he would exclaim: "How I wish I had a man like Moorland on the International staff helping me!"

In October, 1898, his wish was realized, for Mr. Moorland became the second secretary to be employed by the International Committee of the Young Men's Christian Association for its work among colored men. He brought with him a worth-while contribution, for he had gained knowledge, first as an executive and later as an earnest volunteer in promoting Association principles and methods. He also possessed rich spiritual values that he had exercised in his ministry.

The coming of Mr. Moorland into the Association field was a decisive moment—it gave a new rapprochement in service between himself and Mr. Hunton that was destined to make the Young Men's Christian Association a significant and strong social force among colored men.

However, it was not without a very earnest and prayerful preparation that these secretaries began this new era of activity. They were deeply conscious that this larger opportunity meant a larger responsibility and that they were challenged to give an account of themselves. Therefore, they were relentless in their analysis and scrutiny of the component parts of their particular field and its relation to the whole Association movement. They were slow and very meticulous in the formulation of their program. But when these things had been accomplished, they threw themselves with a holy zeal into the attainment of their ideals. No easy, sophisticated prophecy was made; but they started out at that high moment with the abundant physical, mental, and spiritual strength and courage that they knew would be required of them in the stress of succeeding years.

Mr. Moorland had come to give especial attention to the work in cities. Both he and Mr. Hunton would carry on the Conferences. This would enable Mr. Hunton to devote much of his time to the work that had always made the greatest appeal to him. In the student field he found a rare joy, even in the midst of difficulties, that he never experienced in other fields. He had a great

51

affection for students. Writing from Biddle University, he once said:

> It is always a pleasure for me to visit our college Associations, although some of them may not be doing good work. But I meet the fellows and they listen to me so attentively and then they take a new start and push the work for the balance of the year.

He was a prophet and, visioning the future, he could clearly discern that to be prepared to meet it, there would be needed for those then students not only intellectual and physical stamina, but a strong underpinning of moral and spiritual force. The future leadership should be a stronger power than the leadership of his own time—serving under God for the salvation of the race and of mankind generally.

Since Mr. Hunton's death I have met men in many places, busy at their callings, who revere his name for the principles he enunciated while they were still students. These men are convincing examples of the truth of his reasoning. He was ever gracious and had nothing of asceticism in his personality to keep men at a distance, but he could be very grave when there was need. One student said to him:

> Mr. Hunton you can sure give us a good thrashing when you come, but we love you just the same.

To which he replied,

> You usually need it, too, with a little oil poured on afterwards.

His interest in the student field was deepened by the knowledge that in it was the key to the problem of leadership for the Young Men's Christian Association movement, which was already developing with greater speed than the man-power to control it. Here he found opportunity for the careful study of men who gave promise above the average for future usefulness. He found joy in the privilege of laying hands on them for service and, with tenderness but firmness, leading them through a period of groping and searching to conviction and decision. Not all, by any means, re-

52

sponded to the call of the Association, but such an experience left a man with clear and definite aims. However, the strength of the Association even today among colored men is due chiefly to the young men who were touched while in college and afterwards gave themselves with all the enthusiasm of youth to its cause.

Mr. Hunton further enjoyed the student field because there he found the most favorable conditions for the development of the habit of Bible study. I think he would have said with Phillips Brooks:

> I have been led to think of Christianity not as a system of doctrines but as a great personal force behind which and in which there lies one great and inspiring idea.

These were the early closing days of the nineteenth century, when theological opinions were finding a great divergence; when the first deep stirrings of a new religious and social order were being felt by Christian men and women. Mr. Hunton had been under the influence of Dwight L. Moody at Northfield; he was in close touch with the dynamic young Christian leaders of that period, such as John R. Mott, Robert E. Speer, and others; he read constantly and was therefore deeply aware of the religious and social unrest of his times. However, it made him strive but the harder to present Christ as a personal Savior to the students of his field and to make Him so real in their lives that they need not falter in any crisis.

Mr. H. P. Anderson, writing from the International office soon after Mr. Hunton had started this new crusade among students, commented thus:

> My dear Hunton,—
>
> The reports of your visits to institutions in Alabama and Mississippi have been received and have been examined with very deep interest. I want to express to you my appreciation of the splendid work which you are doing in improving the organizations, placing a larger burden of responsibility upon the students and especially in stimulating Bible study. In the difficult field which you have to deal with, it seems to me that you are accomplishing wonders. I wish you to know that we think about your work.

53

A letter written by Mr. Hunton at Tuskegee gave expression to his enthusiasm at this time:

> I would like to tell you everything I have been enabled to do here, but that is impossible. I think this has been the most effective visit I have made here. Yesterday at the two conferences on committee work we got at things thoroughly. Last night I addressed about seven hundred young men on the social life. I believe that had much to do with some sixty young men accepting Christ as Savior in our meeting this afternoon. Some of those were backsliders. Tonight I addressed the whole school, about twelve hundred teachers and students, and I had many personal interviews.

The rapid development of the student field, following this more definite attention given it by Mr. Hunton, soon made it evident that another secretary would be absolutely necessary for any adequate supervision of it, so that by 1905 Mr. Hunton was casting about for a third secretary who would be able to give his entire time to student work.

George Edmund Haynes had in his very early youth won the devotion of both Mr. Hunton and myself. We had followed his student life through the Huntsville Normal School, Fisk University, and Yale Divinity School, from which he was about to graduate. He had often been in our home and we knew him well as a serious student, an earnest Christian, and a leader of men as well as of college Association activities. Quite naturally he was thought of as being well fitted for this new opening. This opinion was concurred in by Dr. Frank Sanders, then Dean of the Yale Divinity School, who knew Mr. Haynes as a student there. Dr. Sanders had also been a close friend of Mr. Hunton since he had first met him in 1893, and was later to become more closely identified with this work as a member of the Committee for the Colored Men's Department. However, first the funds must be raised to finance another secretary for work with colored men.

But raising funds for the maintenance of his work had now been for some time one of Mr. Hunton's major responsibilities to the International Committee. This was done by contact with individuals, large Associations, churches, and other organizations and groups, in parlor meetings. But his most important appeal was made at the Annual Dinner of the International Committee, held in New York. This occasion always presented two difficulties for him. First, the occasion demanded "full dress," which he disliked very much and absolutely refused to wear until after our marriage. Knowing his impeccability in the matter of dress, it seemed rather paradoxical that there should always be required an undue amount of pampering when the wearing of an evening jacket was demanded of him. Perhaps this was one of the few idiosyncrasies that he held until the end. But the more important difficulty was whether, in the light of the fact that many other secretaries had to present their respective claims, he could so present his own work in the few moments allotted to him that his hearers would be able to catch a clear vision of it and realize its full significance to the entire Association movement. It was never a gala event for him, but a moment of deep import to the future of his Cause, and so he always spent some time preceding it in deep reflection and communion. Somehow, these dinners, that brought together all the leading forces in the Association movement and many outstanding persons outside of it, left him rather strangely depressed.

It was probably the fact that until after the coming of Mr. Moorland he was the sole interpreter of his group at these functions, and therefore felt too profoundly accountable. He always wrote about this event at its conclusion if I were not at hand to cheer him.

He once wrote:

> I arrived in New York last Thursday morning and attended, for the first time, the Annual Conference of the Secretaries of the Y.M.C.A's. There were eighteen of the twenty-five secretaries present, representing all the great departments of Association work and coming direct from the scenes of their labor in various parts of the United States and Canada. The conference lasted six hours, from ten-thirty A. M. to four-thirty P. M. A spirit of earnest devotion prevailed and many important matters relating to the general work of the Associations were carefully discussed.
>
> After an hour and half recess, we met again, with the members of the International Committee and some forty of the wealthy Christian men of New York, Brooklyn, and a few

from other cities, at the Annual Dinner of the International Committee. There were nearly one hundred in attendance. I shall not attempt to describe the feast. It was simply all that wealth and sanctified desire could make it. Then followed speeches, or rather ten minute statements of what each agent of the Committee had done during the year. Of necessity there was a good deal of "boiling down." Being the youngest agent of the Committee, I led off, after a few remarks by the Chairman. I was followed by General O. O. Howard, who also spoke in reference to colored young men, but he is not an agent of the Committee. The other secretaries followed in quick interesting statements regarding their work among Germans, railroad men, college men, in general Associations and in foreign lands. Many visitors then spoke. It was a source of inspiration to hear some of them. At eleven o'clock the feast was ended, the feasters having spent five hours in speeches and in consuming the delicious spread. This was certainly one of the brightest days enjoyed since I have been in Association work.

Still later he wrote:

My! But was not that a swell affair last night at the Hotel Savoy. I shall not try to describe the gorgeous banquet hall. It was simply grand. I spoke and felt rather depressed afterwards for I feared I had not done well, although I received a hearty applause two or three times in my six minutes' address and at the end. However, I was comforted, when later on Mr. Morse made reference to my "eloquent appeal," and this morning I am utterly surprised at the way the men in the office speak of my effort. But I will write no more about it.

After one of these dinners Mr. Thomas K. Cree sent him a cheering message in which he said:

Dear Mr. Hunton.

Your presentation of the Colored Department was admirably done last night. It was fresh, interesting and impressive and will help the whole work as well as your own department.

Every year he would receive words of commendation similar to those above, and they cheered him very greatly and in a rapidly evolving situation where there was need of much sympathetic co-operation. He was heartily glad, however, when Mr. Moorland's voice joined his or sometimes spoke courageously and forcefully alone for their department at these Annual Dinners and on other occasions. Mr. Moorland would often jokingly accuse him of wriggling himself out of these state occasions and inveigling him into them.

So it came to pass in 1905, when special financial appeal had to be undertaken, with some success, before a call could be definitely made for a third colored secretary, Mr. Hunton very earnestly addressed himself to the task. In May of that year the International Committee had authorized him so to do. Writing from Brooklyn in June he said:

> I saw clearly that I would not be able to raise anywhere near the full amount this summer. Then, too, I must let Edmund know whether we are to call him. In fact I want to have him with me at Northfield if he is to work with us this fall. All this I laid before Hicks and he said he would recommend that a call be made if I raised half the fund this month or before the call is extended. I, therefore, decided to try Detroit and ask a few people en route who have helped me in the past.

This trip to Detroit led not only to immediate success in the call of Mr. Haynes to student work that summer, but also led the Detroit Association to a permanent interest in this department of the International Committee's work, which expressed itself in a very tangible form a few years later; for in 1909, when he was again soliciting funds in Detroit, Mr. Hunton wrote with joy:

> You will be glad to learn that the Detroit Association has assumed twelve hundred dollars of our budget for next year and expects to increase it to two thousand dollars. This is one of the best things that has come to our department. I will not have to solicit funds here at all, but only to come for an occasional address.

Writing the next fall from Bronxville, New York, where the Staff Conference was being held, Mr. Hunton said:

> Dr. Sanders presided this morning when our work was presented, said many good things and introduced Edmund in a splendid way. Edmund made a very good impression. We are being congratulated on every hand.

57

Mr. Haynes, desiring to pursue his studies further, remained a member of the International staff but a comparatively short period.

Mr. John B. Watson was next to be added to the International staff for work among colored men. He brought not only the richness of his own college life as a Christian leader, but the added ripeness of a young college instructor whose contact with students in this relation enhanced his value. He gave unstintingly of his ability and Christian faith in service both in the student and city work for more than a decade. He finally found the urge for the class room too great to withstand; he was primarily a teacher and eventually returned to that vocation—but not until Mr. Hunton had died. Mr. Watson and Mr. Hunton had a very dear friendship that held fast and firmly until the latter's death.

The flood-tide of those years of widening horizons came with 1908 and 1909. Although Mr. Moorland and Mr. Watson were concentrating all their energies on the work, Mr. Hunton found very little time for rest or to be with his family. In October, 1908, writing from Atlanta, he said:

> I find I will have to go to Montgomery next week. We are so short-handed, and our work is assuming such proportions that emergencies will require frequent changes of program. I trust you will bear with me in this, dear, and try to follow me in heart and prayer.

At that period he felt physically strong and was most enthusiastic if unequal to the demands being made for the expansion of his work. He was travelling constantly, especially in the South and Southwest, with his task very clearly before him. He believed most implicitly that the Young Men's Christian Association movement went directly to the very root of the well-being of men, especially the younger men. He and his associates did not pause to lament their urgent need of a larger and stronger leadership, but labored with confidence and efficiency for the attainment of this ideal.

Although he was extremely busy, this period brought to me some of the most interesting letters of our long correspondence. He was constantly meeting new friends as well as old, and constantly finding new scenes to describe. He could write at great length, and his detailed and intimate descriptions were not only engaging but most revealing of his clear insight, calm and sympathetic judgment, and comprehensive knowledge.

He wrote to me about a great many people whom he met, many of whom I have never seen. He was quick to recognize and to write about the good qualities of an individual, but I can recall but one instance when his praise might seem to approach fulsomeness. Writing from Jackson, Mississippi, he described a gentleman that made so profound an impression upon him that he talked of him very often until the close of his life:

> Was introduced to a Mr. Rischer, a colored business man of Jackson, with whom I spent the evening. Mr. Rischer is a remarkable man. I can say of a surety that he is a high type Christian gentleman. He owns and runs one of the largest grocery stores in Jackson and the largest bakery in the state. He sends bread and sweets all over the state. While he is not an educated man (and he knows it) yet he is a most sensible man and holds a conversation with much interest. He must be a practical business man for he has been very successful. He is a very active member of the A. M. E. Church and secretary and treasurer of Campbell College. He is the poor man's friend. It was great to see him yesterday, as we drove around, speaking so kindly to everyone and everyone speaking so kindly to him—white and colored alike. He is strong in race feeling and is one of the very fair and prosperous men among us who fully identifies himself with his race. He has fine horses, a lovely home and a beautiful wife.
>
> I noticed in his store a fine soda fountain with both ordinary and fruit syrups and wondered whether he sold to colored people. Finally he went behind the counter and not only served me with my choice, but an old colored man and two boys who were wistfully looking on—one colored and one white—before drinking himself.
>
> He stays here during the yellow fever epidemics and serves on Committees to help the needy. Last summer he had the fever himself. When he told me that, he turned and made a remark which thrilled me with admiration. After stating that he had been through with the fever himself, he smilingly remarked "The poor and I are all right now." Well, I must stop writing about Mr. Rischer, but I suppose I shall never stop thinking and talking about him.

In 1911 two secretaries were added to the staff of the International Committee to meet the need of the rapidly expanding colored work: Mr. Robert P. Hamlin and Mr. Channing H. Tobias. Mr. Hamlin had come under Mr. Hunton's influence as a student at Shaw University, and after his graduation entered the Training School of the Young Men's Christian Association at Springfield, Massachusetts. Finishing his course there, he was called to the secretaryship of Washington Association, and a year or two later to the Carlton Avenue Branch of the Brooklyn Young Men's Christian Association. He spent five years there and was greatly loved because of his faithful and earnest service. Quiet, unassuming, but a forceful Christian, he has made a valuable contribution to the Association movement, and all over the country men know and love him.

Until the end, he entered more closely into our family life than any other secretary. Both he and Mr. Hunton were jovial and very much enjoyed the company of one another. There are many pleasant memories of quiet picnics during vacation days and of good cheer and song about our fireside that included Mr. Hamlin.

Writing once from Augusta, Georgia, Mr. Hunton remarked that he had met at a dinner party a young man whom he felt possessed one of the finest and most engaging personalities he had ever seen. He rather lamented his inability to sufficiently impress him with the great importance of the Association movement to arouse in him a desire to enter it. For the next few years he wrote in a wishful and eager way about this young man, Mr. Channing H. Tobias, whom he saw now and then, and finally began to make very definite efforts to secure him as a member of the International Staff. But Mr. Tobias had his own plans for his future and was not to be easily changed.

However, Mr. Hunton's gentle but persuasive and insistent appeal won for the Association movement Mr. Tobias as it had won others, and in August, 1911, he wrote from Washington:

> I arrived on time this morning and have spent the day with Mr. Tobias who leaves tomorrow for Augusta. He is all right and will take hold of student work with vigor and enthusiasm.

60

Perhaps Mr. Hunton's prophetic eyes visioned this young man's possibilities in relation to the Association movement more clearly than any one else, but it is also probable that even he could not dream of all involved in that quiet conference where the challenge was made and accepted.

From the time I first met Mr. Tobias until the present, I have felt him more nearly the counterpart of Mr. Hunton than any one else I have ever known. He, too, has a fine and engaging personality, utter consecration to his work with a tireless energy in the pursuance of it, graciousness and adaptability, save when the relinquishment of righteous principles is involved, and, finally, a deeply spiritual nature, devoid of dogmatism or any assumptions of superiority. It has been a real joy to me to see him for so long a period as a successor of Mr. Hunton at the helm in the Association movement among colored men.

But before his task was finished Mr. Hunton was to have the co-operation of Mr. David Jones in the student field. He came to him fresh from Wesleyan University and brought with him a very winning personality, a virile Christian mind, and a fine sense of humor that was of great value in some of the trying situations of that period. Mr. Jones had great affection both for the work and for Mr. Hunton, whom he nicknamed "Uncle Billy." During Mr. Hunton's illness, he resigned from the staff. At this time the Rev. Mordecai Johnson became a member of the International staff. Both Dr. Johnson and Dr. Jones are now presidents of large and well-known institutions of learning, but both are still regarded as Association men.

By this time, many men whom Mr. Hunton had touched either in college or in his travels had been drawn into the work of the Association as secretaries of local branches. Among these were Thomas E. Taylor, who like Mr. Hunton had been a real part of a thriving Association in his Canadian home at London, Ontario. Mr. Taylor did a great work at Indianapolis and was to be at the helm of the New York Branch in its first big moments. There was C. H. Bullock, at Montclair; W. J. Trent, now president of Livingstone University, then at Atlanta; Robert De-Frantz, now International Secretary, who had served at Topeka, at Kansas City, and finally in the camp at Des Moines, who was always a close friend of Mr. Hunton; H. S. Dunbar, at Cincinnati; H. W. Porter, at Philadelphia; S. C. Burrell, at Richmond; P. A. Goines, at Baltimore, Washington, and the coal fields at Bluefield; George R. Arthur, of Chicago; Rufus Meroney, at Brooklyn. Most of these were preparing without awareness, at first, for a very definite moment of great achievements in their respective Associations. It was to bring to them an amazing miracle in the establishment of a new high that their greatest imaginings had not been able to reach.

Without reference here to the many conferences held, this is but a very brief resumé of the continuously widening horizons of Association work as related to colored men, stretching over a period of two decades, which in its development had the deepest loyalty of Mr. Hunton's life. There were times in his later efforts when he found it absolutely necessary to contend for the principles he had so early enunciated. It tore at his inner being to do so, but he always remained calm and Christian—a positive advantage in time of stress.

He had been separated from his field but three times in all his years of service; twice he attended conferences abroad, the first in London, in 1894, and the second in the Orient, in 1907.

During the winter of 1904 he had traveled extensively and for a long period in the far South and returned home much weakened by malaria that had entered his system. As a result, he succumbed that spring to a serious illness that continued for several months and so devastated him that he never wholly overcame its effect.

The first student Association had been organized at Howard University in 1869. Fisk and Walden Universities had been added to the list in 1877. There were only a few more in 1890. But by 1911 there were more than one hundred student Associations, with a membership approaching 7,000, or more than one-third of the total enrolment of young men in colored schools. These Associations spread themselves over twenty states and the District of Columbia. For their supervision six men had been members of the international staff, though not more than three had served at one time. While many Associations had well-equipped rooms on the campus, Hampton Institute, at a cost of $32,000, had reared the first student Association building.

Testimonials from presidents of a few leading institutions at this time are indicative of the general opinion relative to the value of the student movement among colored men. President S. M. Newman, of Howard University, Washington, D. C., wrote:

> We believe profoundly in our Young Men's Christian Association for the good it has done this year in material assistance, in social life, and in moral and spiritual influence.

From Prof. H. H. Wright, Dean and at that time acting President of Fisk University, Nashville, Tennessee, came this tribute:

> For many years the Young Men's Christian Association has been recognized by the entire faculty as one of the most effective religious forces of the University.

President John Hope, of Morehouse College, Atlanta, Georgia, wrote:

> Negro students, more than any other students in this country, have embarrassing home surroundings, an unwholesome and uninspiring environment within which to earn means to attend school, and are thrown upon their own responsibility. The Negro Student Associations occupy a unique position, doing an indispensable work and giving Negro college men a moral stability and a Christian outlook that will tell gloriously in Negro race life.

Dr. Booker T. Washington, Principal of Tuskegee Institute, Alabama, expressed himself as follows:

> I would like to see the work of the Colored Men's Department, already well begun, extended and developed with great enthusiasm. The co-operation of the better laymen among white and colored men of the South, as well as the North, in this important work of social and civic improvement, is one of the valuable features of the Association movement. I would like to see such a series of meetings as was conducted by the International Secretaries a few weeks ago at Tuskegee repeated in every section of the South. These meetings resulted in the enrollment of a thousand of our students in voluntary Bible Study classes and in the whole School taking a decided forward step in character building.

Mr. Hunton himself wrote in the glow of his preparation for the great Atlanta Student Conference, which he was not permitted to attend:

> It is going to be a great event! I am glad I am being used to prepare for it and that God is giving me the will to work for Him at the sacrifice of temporal comfort and pleasure. I am sure you would not have it otherwise.
>
> It is said of Henry Martyn, one of the first missionaries to India, that the very first record made in his diary after reaching India was "Now let me burn out for God." Oh Lord, would some of us were consumed by such holy zeal.

Mr. Hunton was, indeed, "consumed by a holy zeal" and did "burn out for God."

CHAPTER SEVEN

Culminating Years

1911-1913

THOSE had been brave dreams of Mr. Moorland and Mr. Hunton, in the closing days of the nineteenth century. Under the influence of an irresistible force, they had been drawn together and they had awareness of the fact that, for the time, they were motivated by one indomitable purpose.

This impact, which found in each so vibrant a passion and power to help their fellows attain a social and spiritual victory in this world, was in no sense fortuitous or adventitious. Their training and experience, their elevation above the general attitudes toward life, and their enthusiastic desire to have men realize and appreciate its finest meaning, had for years been preparing them for this convergence of the main streams of their lives—a convergence that would have a deep, as well as a far-flung, reaction in the lives of men. They had no paternalistic motives and they were to be interpreters rather than judges. That Christ-like spirit—imperishable in them—would yield for them the necessary faith and courage.

A decade had been devoted to a careful but rich and broad seed-sowing, for the most part, in virgin soil. There had been also an absorbing and jealous watchfulness to keep away any harmful influence as these seeds germinated. So it was that, at the very beginning of their united era of service, they were confronted with the fact that they had a field ripening unto harvest not only among students but also in cities.

Not only were city Associations that had been formally established calling insistently for help in the rehabilitation or expansion of their work, but there were many budding organizations to be either uprooted or nourished. Therefore, while Mr. Hunton set

65

out to give himself to a larger and more satisfying interest in the development of the student Associations, Mr. Moorland turned with an equal degree of gratification to the call of the city associations. These men together had made a most careful survey of their resources and an analysis of their task, and then, with an acute discernment and a singleness of purpose, they began a serious and noteworthy effort to bring men, through the medium of the Young Men's Christian Association, to a recognition and acceptance of the cardinal principles of Christ's life as a standard of daily living. It was not a vague nor impractical aim, nor a mere experimentation. It was their sincere interpretation of their mission.

But new forces were at work in the world and the dawn of the twentieth century had also been the dawn of a new social service era when men no longer asked the question, "Am I my brother's keeper?" but stood rather bewildered in their new realization of this responsibility for fellowship. Mr. Hunton and Mr. Moorland had hardly taken into account the momentum with which this new social consciousness was gathering shape. It is also probable that their own humility of spirit made it impossible for them to realize the more immediate readiness of their own group to accept the ideals of a new and attractive movement such as the Young Men's Christian Association. The speedy and almost overwhelming impetus that came to their work, especially in cities, was most disturbing to the carefully prepared and satisfying program that they had so recently outlined and approved. They still held to their ideals of city and student supervision; but the exigencies of time, distance, energy, and so forth, often made it expedient for them to do the task just at hand, rather than enjoy the satisfying experience of some previously planned effort.

Even before Mr. Haynes came to help in the student field, Mr. Hunton found himself, of necessity, being drawn more and more into the vortex of city activity. It was the beginning of a memorable period when the words "material equipment" had their first use in the Association vocabulary and the talk about "building campaigns" brought its first awe and enthusiasm. It was indeed a period not only of clearing away the debris of some of the former methods and practices of Associations but also of spiritual re-

66

awakening that would make the Associations more worthily prepared for their rapidly increasing blessings.

Then, because so much of the unexpected was being accomplished, because Mr. Moorland and Mr. Hunton with the authority of the International Committee were doing so great a work among colored men, and because these men themselves had become not only articulate in voicing their needs, but magnificent in supplying them for themselves out of their scanty means, the most significant moment in the life of Association work among colored men was about to be heralded. There was to be compensation for patience and perseverance and a new faith and hope engendered that would pass down through several generations.

It is said that what seems an impossibility for one day or one generation often becomes a reality for another day or generation. Certainly the truth of this aphorism is verified in the history of the Colored Men's Department of the Young Men's Christian Association. Prior to 1910, this department had made no effort to secure very large buildings with large equipment for its Associations. It is true that Mr. George Foster Peabody, ever the friend of the Negro, had given a building costing $20,000 for the colored Association at Columbus, Georgia. Mr. John D. Rockefeller had also given $25,000 toward a building for the Washington, D. C., Branch, and several city Associations had secured for themselves modest but very good homes. But it had been a period of building in spiritual man-power rather than in material things.

However, in 1910, the thrilling and challenging announcement was made by Mr. Julius Rosenwald, of Chicago, that he would contribute $25,000 toward the cost of a Young Men's Christian Association building for colored men and boys in any city that would raise by popular subscription the sum of $75,000. As few if any colored Associations at that time had dreamed of occupying a $100,000 building in the very near future, this announcement of Mr. Rosenwald swept the colored Associations into an amazed huddle for a little while. They emerged with a keener and more appreciative sense of their importance, which, in itself, was stimulating, and it also made for new visioning and new aspirations.

Mr. Moorland and Mr. Hunton were to go into a deep and prayerful consideration of the tremendous responsibility involved

67

in this God-sent challenge. They would be burdened for a while, but would move forward with certainty in the path of outstanding achievement. Meantime, they would find relief in their usual friendly quips at one another and in the assurance that they were being used, in His name, for the expansion of the Kingdom here on earth.

It was but a short time before this that they had given themselves to earnest efforts for success in general campaigns in several cities. Mr. Hunton had written from Chicago early in 1910:

> Moorland has done a great work here. Total amount subscribed—$66,841—nearly all by colored people. Interest is great and general. Besides this there is other good news from this city. Today it is announced that the Chicago Association will contribute $2,500 a year toward the salary and travelling expenses of Mr. Moorland. Big things are happening with us and we will have to do big.

From Pittsburgh he had written a little earlier:

> Things are developing in good shape in Pittsburgh. We had twenty-six leaders at luncheon yesterday and all heartily endorsed the movement. This movement in Pittsburgh is one of the most important we have had.

And then from Pittsburgh, again, a little later in jubilant vein, he wrote:

> We had the greatest meeting here Sunday I have ever seen of colored people anywhere. It was held in the Lyceum Theatre, one of the largest and finest in the city. There were more than two thousand people there, two-thirds of whom were men—a fine looking audience, filling the main floor, first balcony and all the boxes. The speeches were all good, the music superb, the collection taken without trouble, easily covering expenses. Everybody is elated over it and says it was the finest meeting ever held by the colored people here. I have had many congratulations on the addresses I have made here—especially the theatre meeting address. Received a telegram Monday night from Evansville stating that the campaign closed with $1,660 raised—more than half of it cash, and all from colored people. That was great.

Two months later from the same city we hear that—

> Last night was a great night. About 150 men were out to

the luncheon which marked the beginning of our campaign. The hall was packed and the enthusiasm was high, especially when four subscriptions of two hundred and fifty dollars each by colored men were announced. Our report tonight will go much over three thousand dollars. There is a good prospect of our raising about twelve thousand dollars of the three hundred thousand dollars in the city-wide campaign. I received a telegram from Evansville this morning stating that the fifteen hundred dollars cash had been paid in. This is a good record and means much to our work generally.

All of these efforts, that, at the time of their happening, had loomed large, were now to be dwarfed in comparison with the undertakings in special campaigns with the colored men who would be eager to "go over the top."

Of the Philadelphia campaign, in 1911, Mr. Hunton, with an apology for not returning home as scheduled, wrote:

When I reached Chattanooga yesterday, I received a telegram from Mr. Ward, who is conducting the million dollar campaign in Philadelphia, asking me to come quickly to organize the colored men, for they had now been included in the campaign. Moorland will reach Philadelphia this evening and I will arrive there in the morning. The campaign will close next Tuesday. I do not know what we can do in so short a time but we will see.

In fact, he had come so quickly at this call of Mr. Ward, who managed the Y.M.C.A. campaign at that time, that he did not stop at Nashville to get his baggage, left there while making a brief trip to Chattanooga. But his coming did prove worth while, for a building, magnificent for its time, was assured for the Philadelphia Association.

Mr. Hunton did not live to see the beginning even of half of the campaigns inaugurated in response to Mr. Rosenwald's offer, but, during his long illness, he was deeply interested in and prayerful for their success. He had blazed the trail for them better than he knew. It was but a very short time after his death that I stood by the side of Mr. George Foster Peabody as he laid the cornerstone of the Brooklyn Association and paid a glowing tribute to Mr. Hunton, whose services, he said, had made that event possible.

He had passed on, but truly he had cleared the way for "new advantages for his brothers."

Perhaps there is no phase of Mr. Hunton's life as an Association secretary quite so revealing of the man himself as his attitude toward the experiences he had in traveling. Strangely enough, the most trying of these were in his visits to that part of the field to which he was most devoted—student Associations. To me these experiences show clearly not only his rare patience and forbearance but the whole man at his best. He was always so self-contained that he could be in an unhappy situation and yet not a part of it; he was so truly Christian that he could look with pity and wistfulness upon those who shocked his sense of decency and respect; he had a fine sense of humor that could overcome a sense of depression; and he was so much a pioneer prophet that he could endure and vision a better day. I make no apology for quoting at length from letters relating to this large part of his life.

On one trip he made comment in three letters relative to the conditions under which he moved from place to place:

> This has been a tough trip. I sat on the window-sill of the car for three hours before I could get a seat otherwise. The car has been packed all day with a very rough but good-natured lot of folk. We have had fully one hundred railroad hands at different times. Did not eat my lunch until after four. Well, I have survived and will soon be in Charlotte, three hours late. Our next stop is Gastonia.

> There was an awful crowd of colored people who got on in Atlanta going to Goldsboro, North Carolina, to work. They began drinking (women and men) as soon as we left Atlanta. Every seat was occupied—a drinking woman was in my seat. It was awful. Coming down the steps to take the train I saw Mr. Dammels. He said all his lowers were taken but he would try to help me out. And he did. I occupied upper two. Never before have I been rescued from so bad a plight. I was tired. But more than that, I was afraid of that gang.

> I had a trip Saturday night that I will remember for a long time. Forty miles in a freight caboose and four hours late. We had a good fire and all went well. Yes, I know you would have said "don't go." I would not have gone had I known we would have been so late; it was a choice between going on

that train or remaining in Richland all night where I knew no one and then traveling several hours Sunday. All went well.

But it was not always on trains: in the far-off reaches of Mississippi it was much more likely to be oxen carts or floods. Marooned at Tougaloo University, where he lingered after a conference to do some special work, he sent this message after I had been anxious about him for many days:

Here I am still imprisoned with no prospect of immediate release. We had considerable rain last night and the clouds are very heavy today. In fact, it has been raining some. It is past a joke and we are facing our condition now quite seriously. Not that there is the least harm threatening us or that there is the least danger of our being set adrift to forage for ourselves. But Dr. Henderson is thinking of his wife and of his classes at Straight with never a word from either; the Lieutenant is thinking of his home and his mules, wondering whether his wife and his mules are safe and, like himself, taking an enforced holiday; while I, well, my heart is with my family and I also long to be at work. But after all, what poor weak foolish creatures we are. As though our Father could not carry on a few days without us. "All is well."

The teachers gave us a reception last night in honor of our return and are doing all they can to make us content. They have even changed us all about at the table to break up any monotony.

And then:

Red Lick, Miss.

I left Alcorn this morning about ten, traveled sixteen miles in a buggy and was caught in the rain. We sought shelter under a tree, but the rain came down so hard that we put back to the nearest house—a one room cabin where we found refuge. Of course the drops came through the roof. Well, Mr. Ousley had loaned me his rain coat and umbrella so that I did not get very wet. On we came after the rain, three hours ahead of train time. I brought a good lunch with me which I have devoured since my arrival. I gave the young fellow a dollar and he has started back with his mule and his mare rejoicing. This is a slow country, but it is not surprising when we consider that Alcorn is ten miles from the railroad and four miles from the river. I came six miles beyond the first

71

road today to catch the train. At Jackson I shall be in tele-
graph communication with the world.

But not all the hardship was in the South, as evidenced by these
lines, written from Jefferson City, Missouri, after a very hard
journey:

I left Macon, Missouri about ten A. M. and arrived at Mo-
berly eleven-thirty. Had to wait there until two-thirty for
train to Franklin Junction. I arrived there about four
o'clock and had to wait there until ten-ten P. M. for train to
Jefferson City, or rather North Jefferson. Then we took a
bus that brought us by a long rough route over the river into
the city. I then took a cab to the school which I reached at
two-thirty A. M. I had traveled a hundred and twenty miles in
three trains, two hacks and a bus, with cheese and ginger
wafers as my only rations. Well I did finally reach here and
slept well in a very comfortable bed.

He writes from the South again:

Where I don't know in Georgia! This has been a trip,
"sho"! Have made about five changes; traveled on express
and freight trains and bus. I hope I shall never have to come
this way again.

Then from Everett, Georgia:

I am now eighty miles from Jacksonville and twenty-one
from Brunswick waiting for the train from Savannah. I have
been here an hour and have nearly two hours more to wait. It
is an hour and forty minutes from here to Savannah.
I left Atlanta last night in a sleeper and enjoyed a good
rest. Had breakfast before leaving the train; so I am well
fixed. We are in the woods about thirty miles below Jessup.
Pine forests surround us. Only five or six houses are to be seen.
The clouds have cleared away, leaving it bright and warm. . . .
After all there is something to attract attention here. Two
express and two freight trains have passed since I was dumped
here. Then a fellow is busy hauling goods from the depot to
the . . . well, I don't know where he is going, for he is soon
lost among the pines. He drives a yoke of oxen and it is hard
to tell which is slower, he or they.

On this same round of visits to schools, he passed through Denmark, South Carolina, and remarked:

72

I was traveling all day yesterday although I covered less than one hundred and fifty miles. I had to lay over for five hours at renowned Denmark, South Carolina. It was a pleasant, cool day and I walked all over the little town, up the railroad track and up the country roads to keep warm. The people looked at me as if they thought that I was the ghost of that poor fellow they had so recently lynched and feared that I had returned to avenge the crime. I left the town, however, before dark.

I saw a restaurant, evidently for colored diners, where the painted sign informed the hungry that satisfaction was guaranteed. I entered, and there was placed before me black-eyed peas with a slice of pickled pork—all half cooked. Of this I ate three peas by the count. I ate two small biscuits and a fried egg with considerable effort. I paid my twenty-five cents and felt glad to get out. The proprietess followed me to the door with an invitation to call again and with the consoling remark "I am always a little short on Mondays." This I interpreted to mean that her meals were uneatable.

He then related this experience in traveling to Wilmington, North Carolina:

I left Chester at 8 P. M. on the Atlanta Special, Seaboard, and changed to the Carolina Central at Monroe. My! how I wanted to go on to Richmond! There was no Pullman on the Carolina train, so I had to sit up. Slow! It was a mixed train, if you know what that means. The car was warm and there were some gentlemen of Wilmington aboard whom I know; so we made the best of it. We should have arrived here at 8 A. M., but at noon, when we were seventeen miles from the city, our poor engine that had fiddled and fuddled all night gave completely out and we waited for the express train which caught up to us in a short while. Of course, there was no breakfast to be had, except a fairly good cup of coffee provided by the porter. I said there was no Pullman, but one end of our coach was provided with bunks and was in charge of a porter. It was 2:30 in the afternoon when I sat down to a good meal, nicely served, which answered for my breakfast and dinner.

From Selma, Alabama, he said:

I am having a time getting to Tuskegee. I left Vicksburg at four forty-five P. M. Yesterday; reached Meridian at ten thirty-five P. M. and spent the remainder of the night by a good

73

fire in the depot. Had plenty of company and slept some with head on small valise and feet supported by large one while I half lay on the bench. Left Meridian four forty-five A. M. and arrived here at nine. I have been very busy writing on my report, which I expect to finish and mail before leaving Montgomery tonight. I leave here in about one and a half hours, four P. M. and reach Montgomery at seven. Leave there at eleven P. M. and reach Chehaw at two A. M. They will meet me with a buggy and drive six miles to the school.

These, then, were some of the hardships of his calling, and these experiences cited above are typical of similar experiences stretching over a period of more than twenty years. One marvels not so much that his physical strength held so long as that his deeply spiritual nature received no permanent shock.

Before we were married I wrote with some bitterness of spirit, I fear, about some growing evils in travel. He had been in the United States but a short time, with no previous contact with prejudice. But he wrote:

I suppose you think harder of injustices that I have to bear in the South than if you had them to bear yourself. No, Love, *any* other condition would not or might not be better than the present—"sham" though it often is. We must not forget the past. Liberty with a semblance of recognition is much better than absolute slavery. You were feeling hard when you wrote on this subject in your last letter. God is not asleep, nor is He unmindful of what is going on in the United States. Whatever the future may be, you will have to admit that the present, all in all, is better than the past.

You and I will travel together as little as possible in the far South. I can endure many things myself for the work's sake; and I can even suffer your enduring them when it is necessary. But I am sure it would go infinitely harder if we together were subjected to indignities. But never mind, we'll not borrow trouble.

We did travel in the South together, however, and he once argued so firmly and yet quietly that the conductor let us remain unmolested in the Pullman car between Birmingham and Decatur. And when we were taking our dying baby northward to Asheville, his quiet determination again won. These conditions of travel

74

were a negation of the whole purpose of his life. Justice, humane conditions, and enlightened thought were pathetically, tragically missing. But he was never bitter. He was a rare combination—genuinely human with a touch of the divine.

One of the most significant achievements of Mr. Hunton's whole career was in the field of race relations. Both consciously and subconsciously he was ever making an earnest effort to lift human relations above the restrictions of race or creed. He had gathered in his early life an awareness of men that was cosmopolite. He had also learned that real understanding and appreciation of values could create an esprit de corps that could transcend the traditions of centuries, and so he kept his faith that in the brotherhood of man was to be found the true norm of life.

He had a passion not so much for success as for the dissemination of a righteous knowledge among all men; and, because it was clear to all that there were no selfish or arrogant qualities in his leadership, he was conspicuously successful as an exponent of his creed. Whether North or South, East or West, or on foreign shores, his simplicity of manner, frankness in address, and gracious personality broke down barriers of prejudice.

Not so much what men would think of him, but how profoundly he could impress them with his own convictions, dominated his meditations as he again and again faced so many varied groups. His most fertile field for inter-racial development he believed to be among the students of the white colleges and universities, and some of us still cling to that belief.

During his very first summer at the Young Men's Christian Association Training School, Springfield, Massachusetts, when our friendly correspondence had just begun, he wrote:

> I have been quite busy this week, preparing a lecture for today on Association Work Among Colored Young Men. There will be no colored men in my audience, so that I shall have to treat the topic rather peculiarly. In addition to my experience, I have read up on a great deal of printed matter in reference to the work, and, although I have not a written lecture, I feel that I am pretty well prepared. I have prayed that the Lord will be with me.

75

Then from Oberlin, at a later period, he gives his opinion as to the value of personal contact:

> I had a great time at Oberlin. Addressed about four hundred young men Sunday P. M. I had an interesting conference with about a dozen leaders on race adjustment. It was great. Will tell you more about it. I am convinced that one can do much more in a hand to hand encounter with a few leading spirits than in a great public utterance.

As the guest of the Young Men's Christian Association at the University of Michigan, he said:

> Now I must put all my thought on my address tomorrow night. I am to dine tonight with Alpha Phi Alpha, a chapter of the colored fraternity that has organizations in other schools. I shall be glad of that opportunity for a good private talk with our men, since it will give me material, no doubt, for my address.

When at Yale he said:

> The warmth of my reception by the men, this beautiful environment, and the strong comradeship I feel here are all conducive to give me larger freedom in my address tonight.

And so on down to the end of his stewardship, he found much joy in interpreting his own group to the students of another group.

But it was not only in the student world that he was making these contacts. In almost every avenue of usefulness he was from time to time called to throw light on race problems. As for instance:

> I had a very important conference today with four of the secretaries of the Omaha Association, relative to their relation to the colored men of their city. I believe that the Lord used me with good effect. When I get at these men, I do not spare them and I believe the most effective work is done in this quiet heart to heart dealing with men.

To him Mr. Cephas Brainerd once wrote:

> Am very glad you are meeting some of the better class of Southern white people. Such contact is much needed for the best good of both races for it is one of the solutions of the vexed problem.

76

Sometimes it was in conferences that he was given the chance to make a positive advance in the "Christian Way of Life." From the Grand Rapids Convention of the Young Men's Christian Association he wrote:

> Well, the meeting is over and it was a good one. I was allowed to speak nearly twenty minutes. The Lord was with me and I think a real good impression was made. I was fourth speaker, coming after Hodge, Gulick and Ober. Mr. Morse announced after I had finished that, coming to the convention, he met a friend who could not attend. Inquiring about the various departments he noted that an assistant had been appointed in my department and he doubled his subscription of two hundred and fifty dollars for *our* work and also offered $5,000 toward a $15,000 endowment for the support of *our* department. That is, he had been giving two hundred and fifty dollars for the general work and he now gives in addition two hundred and fifty dollars for *our* department.
>
> I received many hearty expressions in reference to my address, from Northerners and Southerners. Not less than six or seven Southern men came and shook hands cordially and expressed their willingness to help me.
>
> A young lady and gentleman formerly of Ottawa came and shook hands. I know both and used to sing in the choir and teach in the Sunday School with the young lady.

Before the International Convention of the Association, held at Mobile, Alabama, he was rather troubled in mind relative to the reception colored delegates would be accorded. However, he went on exhibiting a fine faith and courage in assembling all the colored delegates possible and securing a place on the program for an address by Dr. J. W. E. Bowen. His letters at this time expressed both his hopes and his fears. The happy conclusion was finer even than he had dared to expect. Dr. Bowen carried the Convention with him and his address was printed in full in the leading daily of that city. Nor was there the slightest discrimination in the seating or treatment of colored delegates. In a letter he exclaimed:

> The event is over, closed last night and I feel wonderfully relieved. Our men made a splendid impression on the white delegates, both northern and southern as an article in the "Register" of yesterday shows. I think it is the best editorial

that has ever appeared in a southern white paper. Not an incident happened to my knowledge to mar the general favor with which we were received.

He became associated as far as possible with all intelligent efforts for inter-racial understanding whether sponsored from within or without the race. He wrote of a meeting at Montgomery, Alabama, sponsored by Mr. Booker T. Washington, as follows:

> I am sorry that I did not write to you yesterday. It was a full day. Besides the two meetings of the conference, morning and night, there was a meeting of Colored men at Mr. Crockett's office, called by Mr. Washington to consider our condition and needs.
> The race conference is about what I expected, I say about, for two addresses in our favor were by far stronger than I thought would be made. Ex-Governor W. A. Macorkle, of West Virginia, and Dr. Curry gave these folks down the country, speaking from the broad platform of humanity and justice. What they said, has put, in the minds of all honest thinking men, the other speeches in the shade.
> The attendance is large, especially at night. There were fully 400 colored people out last night, and we had our innings.

He was a most active member of the Southern Sociological Congress, which was really the forerunner of the present very effective Southern Inter-racial Committee.

He was ever ready, too, to be a crusader for the redress of the wrongs inflicted on his people. Whether unhappy conditions could be ameliorated through delegations or not, he thought it a good thing to let the "powers that be" have awareness of the feeling of the victimized group. Writing from Atlanta just when the legislature of that state was about to pass its disfranchisement bill, he said:

> It looks like the legislature will forbid the sale of liquor in Georgia. There is no doubt about their enacting a drastic disfranchisement law. I was before the legislative committee yesterday with a dozen others to protest against the passing of the pending bill. But it did no good. Still we are glad we went.

These experiences of Mr. Hunton, with the added experiences

of Mr. Moorland and other secretaries of the earlier period of Association activity, in their regular and special contact with the white group, give validity to the statement that through the Young Men's Christian Association came the first real stirrings of the present movement toward ideal inter-racial relations. We do not take into consideration here our southern institutions of learning, into which so much of the fine Christian spirit of the North had been poured, but rather that outer world, where men for the most part sat in darkness and cherished their traditions of prejudice and hate.

In the dreamful twilight of his life, Mr. Hunton found a fine compensation for all his sacrifices—all his striving for a true brotherhood—in the letters that poured in to him from many white friends in the South as well as from other sections of the country and of the world.

CHAPTER EIGHT

Conferences and Conventions

FROM its inception, when its purpose and promise were discovered to be too valuable to be kept confined within the walls of that one small room in London, England, where it was organized, the Young Men's Christian Association movement has found in Conferences and Conventions one of the golden means to success. Through these gatherings a way has been hewn out to knowledge, inspired power, high purpose, and true fellowship. Out from them there has ever been an issuance of both higher visioning and deeper consecration, with faith and courage to meet and to overcome apparently insuperable obstacles and to face tasks of unmitigated severity. Along this way a path has been blazed to the great open reaches of a new social order where skies are loftier and of deeper azure and the horizons broader and less nebulous.

When Mr. Hunton assumed the supervision of Associations among colored men, he was at once confronted by the fact that their widespread distribution would limit his opportunities for close personal contact. Such contact seemed very necessary for right development and permanence. Therefore, he must find a way whereby these organizations, very young and very weak for the most part, could grow thoroughly conversant with the principles and methods of Association work and be provided with a program so virile that it would be to these youth permanently satisfying.

While he was making his first tour of the South, the several Associations of Nashville had been brought together for a conference. However, Mr. Hunton felt the need of time for study and reflection before deciding upon any positive or permanent plan for the development of his field. He was using that painstaking deliberateness so characteristic of him in most of his decisions—a deliberateness that sometimes evoked criticism. But to it, no doubt, was due in a large measure the fewness of errors he made either in the judgment of men or of matters, and to it may also be ascribed much of the steady and sane growth of the Colored Men's Department. But as soon as he was really convinced that conferences could be made to fill, somewhat, the wide gap in personal visits, he heartily recommended to the International Committee the holding of three and perhaps four conferences that very year. He then went with eagerness and alertness to prepare for them. From the very beginning, these conferences caught the imagination and interest not only of students but of teachers, preachers, and men in other walks of life. Although International and State Secretaries were the natural leaders of such gatherings, the program was by no means limited to these. In reading about some of those early leaders I have noted such names as the Reverends J. Albert Johnson, Lincoln Gaines, Levi J. Coppin, and A. L. Grant, all of whom afterwards became Bishops; the names of other ministers, such as F. G. Grimke, William M. Moss, George W. Moore, Richard Spiller, and Dr. Mitchell, of Wilberforce, are also listed. Then there were professors and teachers: S. W. Atkins, John R. Hawkins, I. Garland Penn, D. Macon Webster, James M. Colson, Gregory Hayes, Yorke Jones, P. W. Russell, S. A. Johnson, J. M. Gandy, President Johnston, with many others.

Some of the topics discussed in these early groups show a kinship of the problems of that day to those of the present. "What a community has a right to expect from an Association and what an Association has a right to expect from the community"; "How can the Association better adapt itself to the social needs of the young men of our communities?" "What are the young men doing with their earnings?" "The mental improvement of working men, how?" "Social Hygiene"; "Social Ideals"; and kindred subjects were included in a program dealing strictly with Association methods and principles.

These gatherings grew with the years in favor and in strength and were the harbingers of those more intensive and extensive summer conferences—Asheville, and King's Mountain, Chesapeake Bay and Harper's Ferry—that evolved at a later period.

From one of these early conferences, held at Lynchburg, Virginia, in 1892, Mr. Hunton wrote:

> The conference is over. All day yesterday it rained; and last night we had sleet. But our conference was a great success in every way. It was remarkable the way the people turned out. The papers and discussions were good and orderly and every session was marked by its spirituality. All the visiting delegates have gone home and I am helping to raise money to liquidate a debt. In this we are meeting with success.

From Atlanta, soon after our marriage, he wrote:

> This is the eve of our conference and I feel like turning to you for some comfort. I have done a great deal of mechanical work toward making this conference a success, but I realize that I have not been enough with God. All is nearly ready and the young men are coming in. I begin to wonder if they will get the blessing and help they so much need. As leader, I should have had at least three days of quiet preparation and I have not had three hours. Last night and today I have been trying to throw the Conference upon God's hands.

But the success of this conference was finer than he had anticipated, for he wrote at its conclusion:

> I am happy to say that it was successful beyond my expectation, an advance over our Nashville Conference of last year in the number of Associations represented, tone of papers and discussions, and in actual results. Besides the nine Associations represented, including Atlanta Baptist Seminary, there were students from three other schools of higher learning in Atlanta. Presidents, teachers, and students all took an active part and all were highly pleased with the Conference.

He was assisted in this Conference by Mr. J. E. Moorland, who had not yet come to the International Committee as Secretary. Of him he wrote:

> Mr. J. E. Moorland, who was for fifteen months Secretary of our Colored Association at Washington, D. C., and is now pastor of a church in Nashville, Tennessee, ably helped me. He rendered very valuable assistance. I could not have pulled through successfully without that aid.

In 1897, Mr. Richard C. Morse, Executive Secretary of the

International Committee, attended the Conference held at Shaw University. On the eve of this gathering, Mr. Hunton's brief message read:

> Just a note before going to our first session. The men have been coming in during the day and all is ready. I am well and depending upon God for blessing. Who is also my strength.

It was a happy and profitable occasion, and its conclusion brought the following:

> Our Conference is over. I am exceedingly thankful to be able to say that the entire Conference was quite satisfactory. I would like to write you about it all, but how can I? The meeting last night was glorious. The testimonies given as to impressions received, I am sure, showed that a new kind of meeting had been held among the colored people of North Carolina. It was very comforting to me to hear those testimonies. There was not a single incident that jarred the harmony of the meeting, not one point of order raised, and then we had such excellent papers and addresses, everyone to the point, and such full and interesting discussions as to put this conference easily above any other.
>
> The attendance was the largest, about fifty, and then too, we had Mr. Coulter and Mr. Lewis, both of whom made a very strong impression, and Dr. Lee, a white evangelist, was a tower of strength to us and was with us in many sessions. I will tell you about him. And then again Mr. Morse came Saturday afternoon, attended the reception that evening, and Sunday night sessions. All were very glad indeed to see him and drank in his words of warning, encouragement and exhortation. Nearly all met him personally and were delighted with him. I wish you could have been there and heard the many nice things he said about me. It was a little embarrassing as I was presiding, and yet I hope I did not have the "big-head." But better than all else the Lord was with us in power from beginning to end. There were many evidences of blessings received that I cannot mention now.
>
> Dr. Mitchell's address was exceptionally fine, as were Prof. B. S. Johnson's and S. G. Atkin's. All were good, in fact, but these especially so.

The most satisfying of these early events was held at Biddle University. Mr. Hunton saw there the definite growth that had

83

been taking place during a period covering seven years. He was happy, too, because Mr. Moorland had just come to have a share in the work. In contented mood he penned the following lines:

> Our conferences closed last night with a most successful and impressive meeting. It has been the most practical and helpful conference yet held. Dr. Sanders and the faculty are delighted that we came and invited us back next year. The Lord has richly blessed us. Prof. B. A. Johnson is to write a report for "Men" and Moorland and I for other papers. Moorland and I appear often on the program, but it proves decidedly for the best. We were able to draw out the men, provoke questioning, and so secured the practical suggestions needed. The men are all delighted with the method of conducting the conference.

From far off Tougaloo, Mississippi, he wrote, in 1900:

> This is a beautiful day and all our surroundings here are very pleasant and inspiring. Most of the delegates expected have come. Our opening session this A. M. was the very best we have ever had. Dr. Woodworth gave us a happy address of welcome. All our exercises this morning tended to a deep spiritual impulse; and yet there was freedom and humour.

It was at a Baltimore conference of this period that Mr. Hunton reached a state of highest enthusiasm, for he exclaimed:

> Oh! I have so much to tell about yesterday. It was a big day. The men's meeting was attended by six hundred. Reverend Albert Johnson came over and set the men on fire. It was the best gospel address to men I ever heard. Dr. Beckett did the singing, two men professed faith and a number asked for prayer. It was a great meeting, one that Baltimore will not forget in a long time.

It was my great privilege to attend some of these early conferences, where I not only acted as a kind of private secretary but entered with him into those moments of quiet meditation and deep silence that were always a part of his preparation for the sessions.

In later years I have learned these precious lines of Dr. Rauschenbusch; but it seems to me that I had already, in those earlier years, learned their meaning from Mr. Hunton. They read:

> In the castle of my soul
> Is a little postern gate
> Whereat, when I enter
> I am in the presence of God.

Finally came the period of expansion when men came together under the Association banner for longer periods of work and play, prayer and consecration.

All of the places chosen for these conferences have scenic glory. Asheville, North Carolina, away up in the blue of the skies, often shrouded by the mists of the clouds, was first chosen. Then, after a bit, it was at Arundel-on-the-Bay, looking out on beautiful Chesapeake Bay, that tents were reared for the summer sessions. It was a jolly group of men living there close to nature—swimming, boating, fishing, and enjoying other sports, but with all, spending hours in earnest work and devotion. It was really a school, for Mr. Hunton would write of "examinations" and "marking papers."

It was a glorious period for our son—Alphaeus—who had a chance there to be near his father and pal with him for a longer period than at any other time during the entire year. There was freedom and touch with men of the finest type.

Then, during Mr. Hunton's illness, the panorama changed. It was to scenic and historic Harper's Ferry that his associates went, writing and showering him with post-cards from there.

But it was at King's Mountain—held almost sacred by students—that Mr. Hunton found his greatest joy and exaltation in conferences.

In his visits to the students of the school there, he had admired not only the glory of the mountains all about him, but also the glory of its isolation for concentrated contemplation and communion.

It had for some time seemed to him an ideal place for fruitful gathering of students. But although his prophetic instinct had given him a profound conviction that King's Mountain would

85

prove a mount of transfiguration for many, if chosen, yet because of the many considerations involved, he held the announcement of his convictions in abeyance while he slowly deliberated over it and could see with clarity the wisest action. Finally he wrote me:

> Mr. Tobias came up to Charlotte Saturday and we have agreed that Kings Mountain will be the best place to have our Student Summer Conference May 24 to June 2. I am sure you will think so too when I go over all the facts. The major part of my time from now on will be given to the preparations for this most important conference. I want your council, prayers and help, Dear.

This decision held a profundity hardly recognized at the time.

Mrs. Cecilia Sanders, then Student Secretary of the National Board of the Young Women's Christian Association, and I were sent to King's Mountain during one of these conferences. The buildings had few comforts. I recall quite clearly that we kept our lamp brightly burning at night to see more clearly, though with some uneasiness, the antics of our nocturnal visitors—the rats—which made quite a commotion and seemed utterly oblivious of our presence. But when day came, we very quickly forgot those pests and all other inconveniences as we drank in the great glory of those mountains and watched the youth there assembled—fine and earnest in their budding manhood.

Joyously these lads from many a southern school scaled the boulders for their "round-top" evening meeting and, in happy song, sent their fresh voices echoing against those peaks.

There, at King's Mountain, many of these youth caught their first clear vision of the Kingdom of God here on earth and started out with a valiant and glorious faith to find their places in it. The names of many of them—men today—would make an honor roll finer than any one has yet realized. My heart has thrilled many times and in many places as I have seen and talked with the men who were students of that period. To mention one notable example, Max Yergan went to King's Mountain from Shaw University and, having received his measure of consecrated courage, fared forth to far-off India and to East Africa, then to France during the World's War to be a light unto men in the darkness of death and destruction, and, finally, to South Africa to become the

86

pioneer for the Young Men's Christian Association movement there.

Today when I go to King's Mountain for conferences, I find all the comforts necessary to one's physical well-being, but I forget them in my deep longing and prayer that the place shall not lose its spiritual glory. I believe the full significance of the work of the young men at King's Mountain as Mr. Hunton visioned it may be summed up in Paul's words to Timothy:

> Study to show thyself approved unto God; a workman that needeth not to be ashamed, rightly dividing the word of truth.

But these conferences of city and student Associations, held specifically to strengthen the Association movement among colored men, were but one of the factors in this important part of his varied duties. The conferences of the International secretaries, usually held in September of each year, were of utmost importance to him, since they were, very largly, the visible source of the wisdom and inspiration so much needed for the right administration of his own field. These meetings also quickened the urge for that deeper and closer life with Christ, which was always so fundamental and vital to his well-being. His only creedal formula was "to be at one with Christ."

Although the only colored member of these earlier secretarial conferences, he never had one unhappy experience. Yet he did have a great longing for a larger representation from his own Department that often made him somewhat anxious. But he was always thankful for the opportunities and blessings of these particular meetings and the deep and lasting friendships that were kindled between so many of the members of the Staff and himself.

He did live long enough to have those early yearnings for colored associates at these gatherings of International secretaries somewhat gratified. Before he finished his service, five men had been called to be co-laborers with him and to share these seasons of meditation that he had so long and so richly enjoyed.

In 1891 he wrote from Kansas City, Kansas:

> The Convention closed last night. I am detained here for two days attending special conferences of the Secretaries of the International Committee. These conferences are very help-

87

ful to me, for we all unburden ourselves and tell of the difficulties with which we meet and receive consolation and help from each other. I have felt quite alone in my work, there being so few colored men engaged in it. But I have the consolation and strength which comes from a firm conviction that I am where God wants me to be.

From the New York conference he wrote in September of 1893, just after our marriage:

I have just finished my address to my fellow-workers—one hour and a quarter on the department of the work under my care. I spoke from full notes—which I will show you—The Lord helped me.

A little later from Belmar, New Jersey ("Beautiful Sea"), came these words:

Mr. Millar at the close of his statement yesterday morning about his own work, gave in a few words the strongest kind of testimony as to the difficulties of my field and the importance and success of my work, for which I have thanked him. Major Hardie led in an earnest prayer. He has spoken to us several times here about the importance and difficulties of my work and asked me to call on him for help when needed.

But best of all, Mr. Morse walked with me a few minutes yesterday evening and said some most encouraging things to me. When better times come, and they are coming, he wants that my department should be one of the first to have an added secretary. He also suggested a plan and will assist in carrying it out by which we hope to have several colored college men at Northfield next summer. God has blessed me beyond my deserts.

And from the same beautiful place, he wrote again a year later:

A special and new feature of the conference were three papers by Mott on the physical, intellectual and spiritual preparation of International Secretaries. I received three good thrashings and I most sincerely hope that I will profit this year and every year by them. Now don't say "You won't." For that discourages me. I know I go too much and often work too hard, and I *mean* it when I say I will change. I am now going to take time to rest, think, plan, study, pray, and even to recreate, although I will not promise how much for the last.

88

There was always interesting comment in his letters to me from these conferences. In one from Long Branch, New Jersey, in 1899, he said:

> I turn to you with a feeling of joy that we can communicate with each other though far separated. I am feeling very well, eating heartily and enjoying the Conference as fully as ever. Moorland left this morning for Virginia and I am to meet him in Richmond next week. There are but a few people left here in this immense building. To give you some conception of its size I may repeat what Mr. Morse said yesterday. The secretaries of two departments, Railroad and Field, were meeting at the same time, but in separate parts of the hotel. Mr. Morse was with one and wished to go to the other and return. The distance one way was a quarter of a mile, so that he walked a half a mile in going and returning. That is to say the hall running the full length of the building is more than a quarter of a mile long.
>
> Am getting some splendid suggestions here and feel more than ever the greatness of the work to which God has appointed us. I say "us." You have a real share in this work which I trust you will realize more and more and the joy of which I trust will come to you more and more.

Attending one of these conferences held at Princeton Inn, he exclaimed:

> We have been breaking down traditions of race and color here much to the joy of the fine colored men who are servants in this aristocratic hotel.

From Atlantic City, in 1906, he mentioned for the first time the "growth of inter-racial problems with the growth of the work," and acknowledged an increasing difficulty in making his challenge with a very sure forthrightness and yet with such lucidity of vision and spiritual fervor that not only the position that had already been won for his Department would be held, but that there would be new gains.

Again writing from the Conference Room of the International Committee, in 1909, he said:

> I feel that my report was not as good as usual. Yet the Lord blessed us this year as never before. A lady contributed $1,000 toward the salary and expenses of our fourth secretary,

89

and the Boys' Work Committee and secretaries subscribed five hundred dollars toward the salary expenses of another secretary for Boys' Work in our Department. This is simply great.

Apart from these, with a program adapted to the whole realm of Christian life rather than any specific part of it, were the Northfield Summer Conferences. From the very beginning of his service, they had been to Mr. Hunton, each year, a veritable retreat for bodily, mental, and spiritual recreating. Describing a day, he said:

> What have I done today? Let me see: Up at six. Private devotions. Family prayer at seven. Breakfast at eight-fifteen. Wrote a letter and enjoyed fresh air until nine. Attended association methods at eleven, attended Bible study at twelve, and heard address in auditorium at twelve-thirty. Conference with Mr. Morse and dinner at one. Talked a little and lounged about on the grass until three. Took a long walk to the Young Men's Christian Association Camp until four. Wrote six letters. Sat with all the guests at Revell Cottage for pictures. Supper at Six. Round Top at seven. Heard Mr. Moody on "Qualifications for Successful Christian Work" in the auditorium. That is quite a long bill of fare, and you might wonder where my rest comes in. But I do rest somehow. There is such a pure, peaceful, uplifting atmosphere here, natural and spiritual, that I seem to be really resting from my work.

Several years later, writing again from Northfield, it was clear that both his interest and his enthusiasm had been very steadily mounting:

> God has his own method of compelling us sometimes to fall in with his plans for us—and his plans are always for our good. In thinking of this conference, I had never felt that I could spend more than half the time here. But now I have decided, for what seem to be conclusive reasons, that I must spend the full time.

Then from his last conference there:

> Another day has closed. When I think of the many wonderful privileges God has given me, and of what little use I have made of them I feel ashamed and grossly hypocritical. It is a

90

great privilege to be here, and I hope to be a better and consequently a more useful servant of our Lord as a result of my being here and meeting Him.

Dr. Schieffelin gave a very interesting talk on "Round Top" on "City Mission Work" to which he has devoted his life in New York.

Then at the close of that year:

> The closing meetings last night were most impressive. Both were held in the auditorium because of a slight shower that rendered meeting on Round Top undesirable. There was great spiritual power in yesterday's meetings. There will be perhaps twenty in the conference that remains, and all will go to the Northfield Hotel. I expect to get many practical suggestions out of it.

From the foregoing letters it may be seen what a great influence the conferences at Northfield had upon him.

Mr. Hunton was often called upon to attend conferences of special groups of Association workers, such as the one instanced in the following quotation from a letter written at Harvard University:

> The University has not opened its sessions. This is a conference of leading Association men who have come several days ahead of time to set up their work for the fall. There were about fifty young men at the meeting last night, and I heard it said that it was the best session yet held. There were three speakers. First, a young man, named Wanamaker, from South Carolina, who took a post course at Harvard one year and leaves today for China as a missionary teacher. Second, Prof. Chen, a native and teacher in Peking College. Third, your humble servant. I think I made a good impression, I mean for the good of the work. I believe that some financial results will follow up in the near future.

Still another part of this particular realm of Association activity was the Annual Conventions of the Young Men's Christian Associations of North America, that were held under the guidance of the International Committee. They were large and significant events, bringing together hundreds of men for knowledge and inspiration. It was with these early conventions as with other events—Mr. Hunton lamented the absence of colored men. His comment at one of these early conventions was:

> Again I have to regret that I am the only one of my kind here.

But finally in 1897, the International Convention of Young Men's Christian Association met at Mobile, Alabama. I have written about this elsewhere, but so significant was its effect that I quote this paean:

> Praise the Lord for His great goodness. How I have wanted to tell you all about it. Everything infinitely beyond our brightest expectations. Not a ripple of unpleasantness observed on account of our presence. Dr. Bowen was most heartily received and his address was inspired of God. Major Hardie's response was a wonder. Oh! but I can't tell you as I want. Dr. Bowen dismissed yesterday's session with the benediction. I opened this morning's session with reading and prayer. God has wrought wonder here in a day. Praised be His name!

At the Boston Convention Mr. Hunton was happy to have Mr. Moorland with him and also Mr. Booker T. Washington as one of the speakers for that occasion. He said of this occasion:

> Mr. Washington's address was fine. He spoke on Y.M.C.A. work and gave us a great boost. He made mention of Moorland and myself several times, the great good we are doing, and urged the Association to put more such men in the field. Morse, Anderson, Hick and all congratulated us. Will tell you all about it.

By 1908 colored men were beginning to attend these International Conventions, for he wrote in this year from Columbus, Ohio:

> The conference is closed. We had sixteen delegates—as many as I expected. Mr. Washington spoke yesterday to 6,000 people, the largest audience ever gathered to hear any man in Columbus, Ohio, so they said. Three thousand more were turned away from the great auditorium. His presence and address will help us.

92

And from the Toronto Convention in 1910:

> It seems impossible, but I have not had much chance to write you since I have been here. We have nineteen delegates and they have kept me busy. Still I have heard some of the addresses.

In the same year, Mr. Hunton found his first opportunity to address a southern state convention. His comment was:

> Well, my address to the Tennessee State Convention was highly praised, although, when I was introduced, there was not the slightest attempt at applause. They warmed up, however, when they saw I would not bite and there was loud applause and many favorable remarks when I had finished. The paper spoke very highly of the speech the next morning.

Added to these various gatherings already mentioned must be the huge conventions of the Student Volunteer Movement. These brought together from every section of North America students of leading educational institutions and leaders among men. Mr. Hunton participated in these very freely. One of the significant events in my own life was attendance with him in 1902 at the Student Volunteer Conference held in Toronto. There for the first time I saw and met many of the leaders in the Association movement whose names had become very familiar to me. I met both Mr. and Mrs. Morse, lunched with them, and was invited to sit with them in their box during a session. I quickly fell under the spell of Dr. Mott's dynamic power and Dr. Speer's great spiritual domination. I was thrilled by the high enthusiasm with which young men met the challenge for work in the Foreign Field. Also, for the first time, I met some of the secretaries of the then established Young Women's Christian Association, with whom I was to be associated under the new National Board a few years later.

The story of these conferences, however, is not one of complete and constant success. One of the greatest defeats of Mr. Hunton's whole career, and one that carried with it a physical as well as mental depression, was in connection with the Student Volunteer Convention, which met in Nashville in 1906. Nashville had its three Negro universities and a medical college that made an unusually large group of Negro students. They were fine, intelligent, and articulate, which made this failure all the more heartrending. Try as he might and with all the influence that could be used by the International Committee, Nashville refused to give its colored students the freedom of the convention hall, but confined them to a section of the gallery. Mr. Hunton, after doing what he could in preparing the way for those who might decide to go anyway, returned to our Atlanta home for needed quiet and rest.

However, he was not wholly dismayed, for until then the reactions from all these conventions attended by colored men had been to establish a new faith that would help them to withstand some of the future discouragements that would surely confront them. Mr. Hunton, born in an atmosphere of normal human relationships, found the test of the genuineness of his *Call* and the *Answer* in the courage and patience with which he was able to face narrow attitudes and traditions and create a new atmosphere of reason and truth.

London

MR. HUNTON was privileged to participate in three great assemblies of such widespread importance and significance and of such profound effect upon the Associations under his immediate direction that they deserve space in this volume for special mention.

The first of these gatherings was the Golden Jubilee of the World's Young Men's Christian Associations held in London, England, the summer of 1894. The second was the Conference of the World Student Christian Federation that took place in Tokyo, Japan, in the spring of 1907. And the third was the World Student Christian Federation held in 1911, at beautiful Lake Mohonk, in New York state.

The Golden Jubilee in London marked the fiftieth anniversary of the Young Men's Christian Association movement. Its founder, Mr. George Williams, was the central figure of that event and, because of his world-wide and wonder-working achievement in developing a new, unified and active Christian force, he was knighted by the British ruler, Her Royal Highness, Queen Victoria.

94

Being Canadian born and bred, and having acquired a cherished knowledge of British traditions and customs, Mr. Hunton not only felt the thrills occasioned by the anticipation of one's first trip abroad, but was stirred by the knowledge that he would for the first time visit the seat of the British Empire.

May 16, 1894, with other members of the American delegation, he sailed on the steamship Paris and a week later landed at Southampton. Upon arriving in London, he began at once to carry out his plan to explore that well-nigh inexplorable city before the Convention began.

London's treasures in art, sculpture, architecture, and historic edifices, so vast and intricate, were scanned as closely as possible in his limited time. He visited such corners of London as Old Chelsea, made famous by literary celebrities of that and the previous centuries. To Eton he went to see that famous school for boys, stories about which had been a part of his boyhood reading. From Stratford-on-Avon he wrote about Shakespeare, but also about three new graves he had seen, marked with the names of Adam, Noah, and Moses, respectively, with Latin and Hebrew inscriptions below. On the last, he said, was the following sentence: "From Moses to Moses there is none like Moses." Mr. Hunton enjoined me not to let him forget to interpret this to me when he returned home, but strangely enough, I did forget it, and the meaning of the inscription still remains uninterpreted to me, although in later years I have twice visited the great bard's home.

Oxford, with its "Addison Walk," thirteenth century Christ's Chapel, and Magdalen College, with its far-famed library, were all most interesting to him. These are all more or less familiar to this generation, but thirty years ago they were a strange new world to an American traveler.

After the Convention, with several friends, he took a trip through northern England. First they stopped at Chester to see its famous Cathedral, the "Rows," and fine old walls; at beautiful Lake Windermere they rested over the Sabbath day; and then they began their journey through that most picturesque lake region of England. By boat and coach they went from lake to lake and finally took a train for Glasgow, where they visited a few days. Then on again across fiords, lonely stretches of country, and past beautiful Loch Lomond, finally arriving at Edinburgh. It was a beautiful and thrilling adventure that Mr. Hunton always loved to recount.

He was particularly impressed with Edinburgh because, somehow, it reminded him of his own Ottawa. His hotel room in that city had a picture of the Fisk Jubilee Singers on its walls. From Edinburgh he went to Liverpool and York, and these he described so vividly that I needed no guide when I later visited them. Back to London he went to prepare for a visit to the continent of Europe.

Mr. James Stokes had been a member of the International Committee in the United States but had, before 1894, taken up his residence in Paris and become the patron saint of the French Association. He now invited the American Secretaries present at the Golden Jubilee to be his guests on the continent and issued invitations for a reception to be held in their honor in Paris. So to Paris they went, but not without some difficulty, for, it seems, none of them spoke French. But in Paris they were taken in hand by an interpreter who saw to their several needs. Mr. Hunton rather persisted in straying away and getting lost, until he was thoroughly frightened by a certain element of Paris night life of which he had not the vaguest knowledge. He also enjoyed experimenting with French dishes absolutely new to him. In other words, he seems by his letters to have had a real penchant for the unknown.

In Paris he was entertained royally, but I think his greatest happiness was attained in meeting again Professor William Bulkley, who was then residing in Europe. They had a very good time together, and Mr. Hunton spent his last night there with him at the Grand Opera.

There seems to have been always a longing to meet some colored people. Crossing on the steamer to Europe he wrote constantly in his daily short notes to me of "two very lovely colored ladies with a very grum looking man." He was not sure, however, that they were colored Americans. He finally decided to make no advances because, as he said, "the man looked like he might bite one." Once during the convention he hurried through the crowd to greet a colored man whom he had spied, but when he had reached him

96

he found that they could not understand one another. But in London he did meet Ida B. Wells, attended a reception in her honor given by "Lords and Ladies," and was very genuinely proud of her.

Mr. Hunton enjoyed Brussels very much, and there again wandered about losing and finding himself and having much fun. But his letters from all places show how discerning he was and how seriously some of the European customs had impressed him. He particularly liked the stores of Brussels and especially admired the great amount of exquisite ivory they exhibited. But he was not unmindful of its source—nor of the king, whose palaces he had seen, and who tolerated the horrors of the Congo.

Antwerp, the stone fretwork of whose grand cathedral seems as fine and delicate as the finest Brussels lace, was the last city visited, and his last letter, before sailing from that port, embodied a prayer. He was gloriously happy because of the experiences of that trip; his thanks knew no bounds; but he prayed with a deep and insistent appeal that it might all contribute to a greater earnestness and persistence, faith and wisdom, for the work to which God had directed him.

Mr. Morse spoke for the American delegation at the Golden Jubilee, and during his speech introduced the American delegates to the convention. Mr. Hunton made a brief address at the all-American dinner, held during this period.

I have left his impressions of that Golden Jubilee celebration to be told in his own words. He gave an address at Hampton Institute in the fall of 1894, which was published in the *Southern Workman*. The essential parts of that address are given below, omitting descriptions.

Many who are present understand that the Young Men's Christian Association had its origin in the city of London, England, where, on the 6th of June, 1844, the first organization was effected, being the immediate results of a series of meetings that had been held during several weeks in a young man's bed room. This young man was George Williams, then an assistant clerk in a dry-goods establishment. Now he is Sir George Williams, the wealthy proprietor of the same establishment. We have not the time this evening to trace

97

the gradual growth and development of this first Association in London, and the subsequent extension of the work throughout Great Britain, also to Germany, France and America.

It is known to most of you that the Associations of each separate state and province in America hold a convention annually; that the Associations of North America meet together in an International Convention biennially; and that once in three years a World's Conference is held.

It was much more than a World's Conference that your delegate had the pleasure of attending last June in the great city of London. It was a great Jubilee—the celebration of the fiftieth anniversary of the organization of the Young Men's Christian Association. Preparations for this meeting were made on a grand scale and the interest of all association workers was greatly intensified by the expectation that the aged founder of the work would himself be spared to attend.

The wonderful success of this World's Jubilee was due, not alone to the intense interest and earnest zeal of the nineteen hundred and forty delegates who were present, not to the untiring energy of the World's Conference Committee who labored so incessantly for several months in order that every detail in the preparation for and the management of the Conference might be made perfect, nor yet to the hearty welcome and unmeasured hospitality of the people of London; but it was also due to the active interest manifested by the churches of London, by the Lord Mayor and Council of the city, and, last but not least, by Her Royal Highness, the Queen of England.

Sessions were held in Westminster Abbey and St. Paul's Cathedral, and special sermons were preached to young men in nearly three hundred protestant churches in London on the Sunday of Conference week. A grand reception was tendered the delegates by the Lord Mayor of London, for the expense of which the City Council appropriated $7,000. Also the "freedom of the city" was conferred upon Sir George Williams in recognition of the great good done the community by the Young Men's Christian Association. Her Majesty, Queen Victoria, expressed her appreciation of the great work being accomplished by the Associations by extending to the Conference an invitation to visit Windsor Castle in a body, and further by conferring upon our revered leader the honor of knighthood.

98

The opening service of the Conference took place in Westminster Abbey. Here amid long drawn aisles and fretted vaults, surrounded by memories of the noted dead, we listened to the opening sermon by the renowned preacher and statesman, the Bishop of London. This service, being held in the early evening, admitted of another service the same evening, the real, enthusiastic opening exercises at Exeter Hall, the headquarters of the London Young Men's Christian Association. Here were gathered nearly two thousand delegates, representing twenty-two different nationalities and speaking seventeen distinct languages. When Sir George Williams made his appearance upon the platform, there was hearty and prolonged applause. The welcome address was made by Archdeacon Sinclair, who delivered it first in the English, then in the French, and afterwards in the German language. It may be well to state here that all the proceedings of the Conference at the regular sessions were conducted in these three languages. Hymn books had been prepared especially for the occasion, with all of the hymns printed in English, French, and German and with the doxology in twenty-two different languages. It was a common but peculiar experience for a delegate singing soprano in English to have the bass supplied by a German on his right, and the alto in French on his left, and perhaps the tenor in Danish or Swedish in front.

I shall only select a few of the most important events with a hope of giving you at least a glimpse of what occurred.

HOW SUNDAY WAS SPENT

In addition to the sermons for young men that were preached in the various churches throughout the city, special services for the delegates were held at Metropolitan Tabernacle. Pastor Thomas Spurgeon likened the Young Men's Christian Association to the houses of refuge built by Joshua for the wandering and fugitive Israelites. He referred to the marvelous growth of the work in the fifty years, to its protective and elevating influence through its agencies for physical, mental and moral culture and its social attractions, and to the well-sustained fact that the chief aim of the Association is to lead young men to a saving faith in Jesus Christ. One of the most impressive sermons we listened to was delivered at Exeter Hall by the Rev. B. F. Meyer of London, to men only, on the important subject of "Personal Purity and Power in Service." Every available seat in the City Temple was filled long before the appointed hour for services that Sunday evening by delegates

99

and friends who were eager to hear one of England's most eloquent and eccentric preachers, the Rev. Joseph Parker, D.D.

The Lord Mayor's reception was held at Guildhall, a magnificent structure with Gothic roof and windows and a capacity for entertaining over six thousand guests. Here the Lord Mayor's annual banquet has been held for nearly four hundred years. It was evident that every delegate expected to enjoy the honor of having attended a reception tendered by the Lord Mayor of London; but when it was announced that no one would be admitted unless he were attired in the regulation full-dress suit, there were sad and disappointed countenances. What was to be done? Many rented suits, which, of course, not having been made expressly for them, did not fit any too perfectly. There were still a very large number, perplexed about what they should do, when the Lord Mayor came to the rescue. It was publicly announced by the secretary of the Conference that the Lord Mayor had commanded that those delegates who had come three and four thousand miles to attend the Jubilee, and who had no full dress suits should not be refused admittance to the reception. This announcement elicited great applause and relieved many of the despondent delegates.

In the early part of the evening, there was an impressive service in the octagonal council chamber where the "freedom of the city" was bestowed upon Sir George Williams. Afterward, all gathered in the large banquet hall and listened to short addresses by the Lord Mayor, Sir George Williams, Count Bernstorff, Hon. John Wanamaker and others. Later a concert was held in the concert chamber and then the guests were conducted by the Lord Mayor and Lady Williams through the various departments of which Guildhall is composed.

It will not do to pass over Tuesday's sessions without referring to the Thanksgiving service in St. Paul's Cathedral. The eloquent, instructive and inspiring sermon was preached by the Lord Bishop of Ripon, who took his text from the sixth chapter of John's Gospel and the twenty-eighth verse: "What shall we do that we may work the works of God?" This sermon was listened to with profound attention and manifestly stirred the hearers deeply.

DEMONSTRATION DAY

The session of June sixth opened with a special praise meeting, after which the large company of delegates enjoyed a series of short speeches delivered by Christian workers from

100

various parts of the world. The Hon. Mr. Wanamaker presided in a very happy manner. The afternoon session consisted of the presentation of addresses, greetings and memorials to Sir George Williams from individuals, Associations, state and national organizations of nearly every country represented. The greetings from the American Associations were presented by Mr. G. W. Pierce of Ohio, President of the International Convention of Associations of North America.

The most imposing event of the day, and perhaps of the Conference, was the grand demonstration at the Royal Albert Hall in the evening. This great hall, which is circular in form and covered by a glass dome, holds ten thousand persons. Nearly every available seat was occupied on this occasion. A sumptuous lunch was served in the spacious corridors of the hall, after which we listened to an organ recital by Mr. William Carter, who also led a choir of five hundred trained voices in the rendition of several delightful anthems. The special musical features of the evening, however, were the singing of the Swedish choir of seventy-five male voices and the sweet solos by Madame Antoinette Sterling. A display of gymnastic exercises was given by the members of the London Association.

Lord Kinnaird presented to Sir George Williams a bust of the latter, in behalf of the British Associations. Then followed a season of religious exercises in which many brethren speaking various languages took part. We shall never forget the baptism of inspiration which came to us as we joined those thousands in offering the Lord's Prayer and singing "All hail the power of Jesus' name."

For a moment caste and class distinctions seemed wiped out, and the kingdom of Christ seemed truly what we know it to be, *a Brotherhood of man,* as rich and poor, high and low, Swede, Italian, American, Australian, divers kindred, tribes, nations and tongues, standing shoulder to shoulder, swayed by one impulse, poured out one prayer to "Our Father" and one praise to "Jesus" in many languages.

Appropriate addresses were made by Count Bernstorff of Berlin, Prince Oscar of Sweden, Canon Fleming, Dr. Parker and others. The program concluded with a pictorial exhibition of the rise and growth of the Young Men's Christian Association, given by the aid of pictures thrown on a great canvas stretched across the auditorium.

As wonderful and as impressive as were the sessions and services of this World's Conference and Jubilee of the Young Men's Christian Associations, something that can scarcely be estimated and explained, would have been lost, if we had missed the unique, but grand, demonstration at Windsor Castle, for here was added to the warm hospitality of the English people and clergy—which so plainly expressed their hearty approbation of the work—the gracious and approving benediction of England's Queen, manifested in an exceptionally liberal and unusual way. Nature seemed quite as glad as the three thousand delegates and friends who wended their way, in sections, by rail to the home of the English royalty. For the sun which had been hidden behind the clouds for several days, shone brightly and permitted the vast throng to view the landscape of Windsor outlined upon a clear and beautiful horizon. The visitors were divided into four sections, distinguished by the colors worn, viz., red, white, blue and green, and were courteously received by the Mayor of Windsor, while the Mayoress held a reception during the afternoon.

Time will not permit us to more than mention the beautiful and interesting features of this day, for these things in themselves would form a lecture. But we sauntered down the Long Walk, filed slowly through the magnificent Mausoleum, where rest the remains of Prince Albert and where there is a mournfully touching space left that will some day (we hope not soon) be occupied by all that remains to earth of England's Queen. Only once a year—on the anniversary of the death of the Prince Consort—are visitors allowed in this tomb, and never before had the Queen given permission for any party to visit it except on that day. We were conducted through the Royal farm, garden and dairy, through the state apartments, Albert Memorial Chapel, and St. George Chapel.

Lunch was served in a pavilion on the Castle grounds and Mr. Wanamaker proposed in a graceful speech a toast to the Queen. Again, by special permission, the Jubilee party was photographed on the Queen's private garden terrace.

Although the holding of any meeting inside the Castle walls is strictly prohibited by law, permission was granted by which the farewell meeting was held just inside the gate. Here all the four sections came together as one great body, and short addresses, resolutions of thanks to the Queen, and of sympathy and appreciation for Sir George Williams, who had become indisposed, were made. This meeting, one of the most remarkable and impressive ever held by anybody, marked the close of the World's Conference of 1894 and the fiftieth anniversary of the organization of the Young Men's Christian Association. The good-byes were said under the walls of "Britain's Royal homestead"—good-byes that would last with many until, as the redeemed of the Lord, all would be assembled inside the royal gates of the Heavenly King, to sound his praises forevermore.

Tokyo

FROM Northfield, Massachusetts, where he was attending a conference in June, 1903, Mr. Hunton wrote me this rather startling letter:

At the Lakewood Conference, Mott told me that he wanted to see me here about something very important. Well, I saw him this afternoon, and while it is not yet quite certain, it is very probable that I am going to Japan next year—yes. JAPAN. The World's Student Christian Federation is meeting in Japan in September 1904 and Mott wants me to go with the half dozen men from America. He is to raise the money and will be able to let me know definitely when we meet at Princeton in September or very soon thereafter. But he says there is hardly any doubt about my going. Well, that is a wonderful prospect. It involves my preparing two or three strong addresses and a paper that will be printed and these make a great deal of close reading necessary for the year before me. Mott, in the fall, is to outline a syllabus for me. My wife, this is a mighty big contract. I could not show the white feather. I told Mott that I know of nothing to hinder my going, and that I would lay myself out enthusiastically in preparation. He has talked it over with Mr. Morse only. It all seems too good and too great to happen. But I am not faithless. Yet, I think it best not to say much about it until after I meet Mott again in September.

One thing, dear, I know; that is, I ought to be a much better man than I am. When I think of all the splendid opportunities I have, I feel that I do not make nearly the use of them that I ought. I certainly mean to guard myself more closely.

I was made so eager by the foregoing letter and was so desirous to talk over this suddenly new anticipation with Mr. Hunton that

103

I wanted one of us, no matter which one, to fly to the other. However, I had to be patient and wait for vacation days, and when they came we talked about hardly anything else. We dreamed new dreams and read with great avidity all that we could find about the Orient and especially about Japan.

To Mr. Hunton as well as to me it was a thing much too stupendous, much too sudden, to be easily conceivable. Vacation days soon ended, and in September from the International Secretaries' Conference at Princeton, New Jersey, came a second word on the subject:

> I had a good talk with Mott this morning on how to prepare my address and paper for the Japan meeting. He gave me a good outline and many valuable suggestions. It will keep me busy all the year in making the investigations necessary to the writing of my paper. I am glad of that especially for the fund of important information I will gather and for the intellectual benefit that will result in the process.
>
> Lewis, our secretary for Shanghai, China, who is home on a furlough and will return shortly, has given me a very cordial invitation to be his personal guest in Shanghai, where I will have to stop en route to Japan.

However, the World's Student Christian Federation Conference did not take place in 1904 as had been anticipated. The Far East was uptorn by foreign war and internal conflict that made necessary the postponement of this great event. This delay was very fortunate for Mr. Hunton, for he was desperately ill in 1904 and would have missed what later proved the most broadening and strengthening experience of his entire life. He had learned the value of the contacts and wider horizons to be gained in travel, but he also knew that he could not begin to grasp the significance of a trip to the Orient in which such a high purpose was involved.

When it was eventually decided that the Conference would be held in 1907 at Tokyo, and further announced that Mr. Hunton had been one of the men selected to address it, I think that, rather paradoxically, we experienced a feeling of awe and elation at the same moment.

While carrying forward his own work in a fast evolving period,

Mr. Hunton gave a most exhausting amount of time for almost two years to gathering data for this address, which was to be world-wide in its reference to the religion, education, and economics of the African world. It was a large order, requiring not only much research but consummate skill in the selection and arrangement of the material to be used. But he worked in the painstaking and patient manner so characteristic of him. Yet 1907 came almost too quickly.

The previous year had brought to Atlanta, Georgia, one of the worst race-riots that have stained the pages of southern history. Mr. Hunton had selected that city as the center for his southern work, and we had been living there for eight years, rearing our two children, who had been born to us there. We had passed through the riot and seen the utter heartlessness of its perpetrators and the passivity of the local government meanwhile, so that Mr. Hunton insisted he could not go so far away and for so long a time, leaving his family unprotected in such an environment. This handicap was removed when, a few weeks before his departure, we took up our residence in Brooklyn, New York.

Mr. Hunton left New York February 22, 1907, made his way slowly across the continent, and finally sailed, March 8, from San Francisco on the Canadian Pacific Line. This trip to Japan was to be an adventure in high Christian faith and courage, a seeking for the enrichment and expansion of God's Kingdom here on earth.

From the time he left New York until his return in June of that year, Mr. Hunton kept a faithful diary. It is a very lucid picture of the scenes and experiences of that grand adventure. Some time later, when the opportunity also came to me to cross the Great Divide, I purposely chose the route that he had taken, and thereby fulfilled *his* wish that I might see the glory of the great Golden West. There was an added thrill in seeing mountains, lakes, and gorges that he had so vividly described in both his letters and notes; and when, at last, I stood looking out past the Golden Gate to the beautiful Pacific Ocean, I felt very close to him in spirit.

Halfway on his journey across the Pacific the ship stopped for a day at Honolulu. Of that blissful day, March 16, Mr. Hunton wrote as follows:

We had a delightful day, yesterday, in Honolulu. Every moment of the time was enjoyed in a succession of strange sights and experiences. Mrs. Crockett was at the steamer to meet me. I was very glad to see her. We went through the very interesting fish market to the Young Men's Christian Association where I left her for a while. Our party then had a drive. The sights of Honolulu! How shall I describe them? I cannot. We drove to the Pali, seven miles up the mountain, where we had a view that I shall never forget. Many say that it is the finest view in the world.

I then went to lunch with Mrs. Crockett. She is stopping with Captain Lorenzen, a German married to a beautiful Hawaiian. There I enjoyed high-class native life with some native dishes that I would not have had at a hotel. We then visited the aquarium, where are to be seen the most beautifully colored fish extant. It was wonderful. We saw an old native church, built of coral blocks, and went through the palace which is now used as a state house. Both branches of the legislature were in session, and I was introduced to some of the members.

After buying and mailing cards, looking in shop windows and at folk, who are all racially mixed to a puzzling degree, it was time to return to the ship. That day in Honolulu! Well, it was glorious. I cannot begin to describe the gorgeous beauty of the tropical trees, plants and flowers and how those strange, happy people impressed me, to say nothing of the wonders of Pali, "Punch Bowl," and the aquarium. Honolulu will always be a name full of charm for me.

Mrs. Crockett says that Mr. Crockett insists that I must stop off a boat on my return and visit Maui and the volcano.

Mr. Crockett had moved to Hawaii from Alabama several years before. En route north, he and his family had been our guests. First he had practised law in Honolulu, but at the time of Mr. Hunton's visit he held an official position on the Island of Maui, which prevented him from joining Mrs. Crockett when she met Mr. Hunton.

Now they were on the second and last lap of that long journey. There would be no more stops until they reached Honkow ten days later. Then from Tokyo he finally wrote:

106

To My precious Wife:

You see I am *here*. A steamer leaves for America tomorrow and I must send you another letter. We did not spend much time in Yokohama, because arrangements have been made for us here and a Secretary was at the Steamer to meet us. My! But this has been a *great* day. Country, people, customs, everything and everybody so new and strange. Cannot describe my first impressions. My first ride in a jinrickishaw was a delightful experience. One of the ladies said she would like to ride in a jinrickishaw all her life.

The Conference of the World Student Christian Federation, in which to participate he had traveled so many thousand miles, was now being held. He said:

The sessions are wonderful. The speeches peculiarly helpful and inspiring and the spirit of the meeting very deep and inspiring. It is always necessary to hurry to get a seat and we rarely get back to our rooms until after the evening session.

Today we had luncheon at the Imperial Hotel, tendered, by Mr. Woodward and Mr. Sleman of Washington, D. C., to all the International Secretaries and their wives who are here. There were thirty-eight persons at the table. It was very fine and enjoyable—a big contrast to the luncheon I had yesterday at a Japanese restaurant.

I have just come from a reception at the home of Viscount Hayashi, Minister of Foreign Affairs, and have a few minutes to write you before the P. M. session. The reception was as fine an event as could have been held in anybody's home in any country. In going through the spacious rooms most elegantly furnished, the Viscount and his wife, dressed in European costume, received each visitor with royal grace. Then we passed into the spacious dining hall for luncheon. And what pretty things they had for us to eat. Meats, cold in many forms or styles, jellies, custards, cakes, sandwiches, fruits, coffee, lemonade, cocoa, etc., etc., and some Japanese delicacies that were fine.

Again:

I have just come from a most delightful garden party given by Baron Goto and, as soon as I write this note, will go to the Methodist School to a banquet marking its twenty-fifth anniversary. This will be the last function of the Conference.

107

Mr. Hunton brought home with him from Japan a solid silver box, bearing the crest of Baron Goto, filled with candy, pin-point in size. This silver box, a two-inch cube, was encased in another box of precious wood and tied with a silken cord. One of these boxes was presented by Baron Goto to each of his guests at that garden party. To the end of his days, when he happened to remember it, he would present to the friends who came to see us bits of this candy.

But it was the conference itself that had the largest place in his mind and heart in the midst of so much luxury and so much strange and compelling beauty.

The addresses, especially those of Mr. Mott and Mr. Eddy, steadied, enriched, and emboldened his spirit. They would be of great value to him in further adventure in his own field. He marveled at the patience and endurance of those who would sit hour on hour intently listening to the message of Christ. He lamented the scarcity of messengers to the waiting millions.

Then the time came for his own address. He had worked on it each day while crossing the ocean en route to Japan. Four days out from Yokohama, he wrote:

> I read my paper yesterday to Mr. Farquahr and this morning to Mr. Beach. Both pronounced it *very* good and offered suggestions for cutting it down without losing any of the contents.
>
> I was especially gratified with Mr. Beach's commendations on my paper. He is the author of that Missionary Geography and Atlas I bought and is thoroughly competent to judge. He said there will not be another paper at the Conference as clearly and logically arranged and couched in such choice English. But I am still working on it and know that an important thing will be to deliver it well.

And then, April eighth:

> Well, I delivered my address to a very attentive audience. Have had compliments on every hand. Mott said I had given the strongest paper up to Saturday morning.
>
> I was made very happy today by Mr. Morse. He heard my address and I had not met him since face to face. He came to me at the garden party and shook my hand warmly and expressed high appreciation of my address. He said it was the

only address that made him cry, and that I had opened even his eyes to encouraging facts. He also said that my paper must be published in New York in pamphlet for careful distribution.

At the close of the Tokyo Conference, the delegates of the Occident were sent out in small groups for short missionary tours through Japan. In earnest prayer and contemplation they made ready to herald abroad the transforming power of the gospel of Christ. From Mito on this important journey Mr. Hunton wrote:

Four of us left Tokyo yesterday morning with an interpreter on an evangelistic tour of six days. We had two meetings yesterday and will have two today. Mito is in the country— although it is a city of 35,000 people. No street cars, no lights —but chinese lanterns—no horses—a large country town. Two of us are stopping with a missionary who has a Japanese home. It is all so strange and pretty—just like a big playhouse. My companion is six feet, three inches tall and is constantly bumping his head. I barely escape. Yesterday— although we arrived at noon—I put on and took off my shoes six times. It was a nuisance. It is now ten o'clock, and I have not had on my shoes yet, and will not until I go into the street. This fine life—but I would enjoy it for a while only.

Our meetings yesterday were largely attended, especially by young men students. The afternoon meeting lasted from two-thirty to five and the evening meeting from seven-thirty to ten-thirty. These folks will sit on their feet half the day to listen to missionaries. I don't see how they endure it—not the addresses, but the long sitting.

Tomorrow we go in another direction. I am getting a chance to see a section of the country that I could not have seen otherwise.

These people we are stopping with are "Friends." They are very fine and have a lovely, sweet home-life. Mrs. Binford is a great worker and was one year at a school for colored students in Arkansas.

This house has two hundred and sixty-five sliding doors.

Then from Kyoto came the following word:

The past four days have been a rush. In six days we conducted eleven meetings in three cities with an attendance of from two hundred to four hundred. The meetings were remarkable in many ways. The people seem anxious to have the gospel, although they are slow to change from their old faith to Christianity. We had several to take a stand for Christ, including a Buddhist priest.

The officials of the public schools of the provinces of Shidzuoka invited us to address a meeting yesterday afternoon under their auspices. Of course we accepted and spoke of the educational work in India, Germany, and America. There were four of us at Shidzuoka Saturday and Sunday. This was a notable gathering of the leading educators of a province. We were most cordially received and highly honored. We told of educational work and preached Christ. Missionaries say that such a meeting had never been held before in Shidzuoka. They presented each of us with a small piece of lacquer work as souvenir.

I came here tonight and will spend two days here. Then go to Nara and to Kobe, whence I sail Thursday for Shanghai. Am very well and enjoying everything.

Oh! I want to tell you that at Chiba, where we were holding meetings, we slept in a genuine Japanese home with Dr. Segawa. That was the most pleasant experience we have had. The home is most beautiful and we slept in genuine Japanese style—including tea before retiring. It was great to be sitting and sleeping on the floor and to be admiring at every turn some new wonder in that beautiful home. We could have stayed there a month.

Met some missionaries from Canada yesterday and was entertained by a family from Michigan. Big time! I plan to spend a day at Shidzuoka next month en route to Yokohama. There is much to be seen there.

Kyoto had been the capital of Japan at one time, and its old palace was still a show place. In that city Mr. Hunton saw his first Cherry-Blossom Dance, which he said was a strange but fascinating pageant. Stopping at Nara, a small town, and at Shidzuoka, that offered much of interest, he went on to Kobe to take passage for China. He made several addresses in mission schools there, and then sailed, March 20, on a Nippon Yusen Kaisha liner for Shanghai. This ship went through the Inland Sea, calling at several ports before reaching Nagasaki, where there was a day ashore before starting on the longer journey across the Yellow Sea.

Mr. Hunton's first letter upon arriving at Shanghai was one of exclamations:

The people, the people! I can understand already somewhat the cause of the fear of the "yellow peril." Hundreds of men striving with each other for a job for which they will receive a penny. Dirty, half-clad men. Awful! And they say that Shanghai does not represent China. Well! I am glad I have had this half-dose as an introduction.

A Metropole Hotel man met our steamer with a list of visitors who were to stop there. My name was on the list. I was glad to turn my baggage over to him and thus escape a siege of carriers who thronged the ship in spite of the attempts of the *Indian* police to keep them off.

In Shanghai the China Centenary Missionary Conference was in progress and here, as there had been in Tokyo, were assembled many earnest Christian men from many places. Mr. Hunton was much impressed by this conference and attended the sessions five days, at the end of which time he wrote:

Sorry that necessity requires that I go now. The spirit of this conference is wonderful. *Unity* is in the air and almost fills it. Brains in the far East are getting together and their action will have a decided influence upon brains in Europe and America.

While in Shanghai, he was the guest of the Y.M.C.A. Secretary and his wife, Mr. and Mrs. Lewis, both of whom won his deep admiration. He had to attend many functions there and was forced to don that unappreciated "full dress suit" very often. But those teeming, noisy crowds of hopelessly poor and untutored Chinese, whom he was seeing for the first time, drew very heavily upon his sympathy there at Shanghai and through all of his travels in China. He said, "I visited the Chinese city. Horrors! Words will not describe what I saw there."

When he sailed from Japan for China, he had no set plan of travel beyond his visit to Shanghai. On the ship, however, he met Mr. Backhouse, an Englishman, who had also been a delegate to the Tokyo Conference. They decided to see China together. They then made a plan to go to Peking by way of Hankow and return to Japan by way of Korea.

Leaving Shanghai by steamer, they sailed six hundred miles up the Yangtze River to Hankow, calling at Nanking, Guankin, and Wu-hu.

When they reached Hankow one evening, not a single room in the hotels was available. However, the proprietor of one hotel arranged for them to spend the night in a luxurious suite on a French steamer anchored in the harbor. Across from Hankow was the larger native city of Wuchang, of which Mr. Hunton wrote several pages. They were now at their farthest point west and would travel by rail due north to Peking. Of this visit I shall let Mr. Hunton speak:

> I have actually been to Peking—and a rushing time I have had since arriving in that interesting city. Mr. Gailey, Secretary of the Young Men's Christian Association at Peking, met us at the station, sent our baggage on and took us sightseeing at once. It was very thrilling to go over the ground where the great conflict with the Boxers was waged in 1900. As we went, I recalled with great distinctness the address to which we listened by Dr. Arnent at Toronto, during the Student Volunteer Convention, when he so graphically described the siege of Peking. In Peking we also visited the Temple of Heaven, the Imperial City (not the Forbidden City), and other temples, towers or scenes of great renown.

Of his visit to Tientsin he wrote:

> Secretary Robertson met us at the station and took us sightseeing at once en route to the Young Men's Christian Association, where we had a semi-Chinese-foreign lunch. Again we rushed about from school to temple, etc., and left ourselves just half the time needed to hurry to our hotel and *dress* for a Chinese feast with Dr. Su, President of the Military Medical College. There were just eleven gentlemen at this feast. I will never forget it. Mr. Woodward, Mr. Sleman, Mr. Backhouse and myself as guests, Secretaries Gailey of Peking and Robertson of Tientsin, President Su and two other Chinese physicians. We had more than sixty dishes and ate ourselves nearly sick. Mr. Woodward says that was the best dinner he ever had.

Later he wrote:

> Yesterday noon we got over the bar and out to Sea. We spent a few hours at Cheefoo, our last stop in China, where I

bought a lace collar for my precious wife. We are now crossing the Yellow Sea and will reach Seoul tomorrow afternoon where this letter will be mailed. We are having good sea and all are happy.

Have I told you who *we* are who are traveling together? Well, I really am traveling with Mr. Backhouse.

When we left Shanghai we found ourselves on the boat with Mr. Woodward and Mr. Sleman of Washington; and at Hankow we were joined by five ladies: Miss Conde and Miss Taylor of the Young Women's Christian Association, Miss Paxon of the Student Volunteer Movement, Miss Rouse of the English Young Women's Christian Association, and a Miss Sheppard, a missionary to Japan. All being directly or indirectly Y.W.C.A. folks and all covering the same territory, we find ourselves met at stations and cared for by the same friends. Several other European delegates are on this boat. We will separate in a day or two, to go our different ways in Korea and Japan and to take different boats to America and Europe. Mr. Backhouse and I will remain together a while in Japan as we each want to go to the same cities.

Back in Japan, Mr. Hunton said of Korea:

Korea has not as many things of interest to be seen as China or Japan. But to see the people and to contrast them with the Japanese and Chinese is both interesting and profitable.

I went to church Sunday night and got a touch of the wonderful religious work in progress in Korea. Next day we studied the political situation and the industrial and homelife of the people. Also visited one of the old palaces and spoke at a big reception at night. The Koreans impress one as being a feeble people, unless it is their broken spirits I see under the unwelcome domination of Japan. Marquis Ito is the real King of Korea.

The trip on the railroad through Korea yesterday was full of interest. The people seem to be living a very simple life, using implements and methods in farm and domestic life that are two thousand years old.

Nikko, the loveliest city of all Japan, had to be seen, of course. The Japanese have an expression that runs thus: "Never say kekko (splendid) until you have seen Nikko." Its architecture is so beautiful and its plants and flowers so gorgeous and varied that

113

it is a dream city. Mr. Hunton said nothing in the world could be more enchanting than Nikko.

This journey had been for Mr. Hunton a rare and marvelous experience. He had seen the sacred and famous Fujiyama; he had been there in the far-famed cherry blossom season, lovely beyond any description; he had seen temples; priceless treasures of a great variety; and finally, he had penetrated to the very heart of China, crossed the great Yellow Sea, and had come again to Japan by way of Korea. When this great adventure had been completed and he was again in Tokyo making ready to move on to Yokohama as the first step toward home, he wrote his final word in that far-off East:

> Above all the enchanting strangeness of this land and its people; above all the loveliness and misery I have seen; above all the sacred grandeur of Fujiyama and the adoration of the Great Buddha; and above the vastness and mysteriousness of China, I see the hand of God, working out His purpose through His servants for the salvation of this old civilization.
>
> Pray, dear, that the meeting here of His servants from the four corners of the world shall yield abundantly for His Kingdom here in the Orient.

Lake Mohonk

IN THE latter part of the nineteenth century, when social service ideals were beginning to find definite expression, a man of God, filled with this new spirit, sought a retreat for quiet conferences. He happened to be especially interested in the welfare of the American Indians and wanted to so interest others. Casting about for such a place as he had envisaged for his meetings, he found beautiful Lake Mohonk, in New York state. It was more than twelve hundred feet above sea level, nestling close to Sky Top Mountain, one of the highest peaks of the Shawangunk Range. It was also far removed from the din of the work-a-day world. On the very edge of one side of this lake he had erected the lovely and spacious Lake Mohonk Mountain House with its gables and over-hanging balconies that cast shimmering reflections on the lake below. The whole environment has a touch of magic fairyland loveliness. Lake Mohonk soon became famous for its confer-ences, not only on the Indian but also on world arbitration and a great variety of other important matters.

The Tokyo World Student Christian Federation Conference in 1907 had been held at the flood-tide of Japan's beauty—the far-famed cherry blossom season. Two years later, another confer-ence had assembled on English soil, within the confines of historic and stately Oxford University. And in 1911 the scene had been completely changed again when the conference was held amid the Byzantine grandeur of Constantinople. Each of the above-named places possessed its own peculiar charm and each represented a widely different civilization; but in their Christian unity they were invaluable to the expansion of the Federation movement.

Then came the Conference of 1913, on the American Conti-nent. The place chosen was Lake Mohonk, and, although very different in character from Tokyo, Oxford, or Constantinople, it held no less charm or was no less fitting for such a gathering. Three hundred and eighteen delegates, representing forty differ-ent countries, met in the Lake Mohonk Mountain House for a week, for the tenth Conference of the Federation. Cognizance would be taken of the progress made, difficulties to be faced, and new plans to be made in the pursuit of the ideals of the movement.

The aims of the World Student Christian Federation are, briefly stated,

> To collect information relative to the religious conditions among students; to unite student Christian movements or or-ganizations throughout the world and to promote mutual rela-tions; to lead students to become disciples of Jesus Christ and to deepen their spiritual life and to enlist them in the exten-sion of His Kingdom throughout the world.

To be better prepared for this highly important and difficult evaluation of their mission, many of the foreign delegates had reached America several weeks in advance of the Conference and had gone in groups under the guidance of home secretaries into the North American student field. They made acquaintances, studied manners and customs, observed methods of work, and made informing and inspiring addresses. Three very prominent foreign delegates were assigned to Mr. Hunton for visitation in his field. They went with him to some of the Negro schools and to a summer conference, and all seemed richly blessed because of that experience.

Just before going to Mohonk, all the delegates were the guests of Mr. and Mrs. Cleveland H. Dodge and Miss Grace H. Dodge at a garden party. It took place on their estate, Greystone, at Riverdale-on-the-Hudson, a place very dear to the hearts of all Association people. This event was really an acquaintance party and was made colorful not only by its lovely setting, but also by the variety of nationalities easily recognized. Mr. Hunton was there leading the colored delegation; and it was only the words "United States" written against the names on their badges that made the colored American delegates distinguishable from some of the foreigners.

Sunday was spent in visiting the various churches in or near New York, many of the foreigners making addresses to the various congregations, and Monday, June 2, the whole party started by way of the Hudson River for the Conference. The steamer landed the delegates at West Point, where, by order of President Wilson, a special dress parade in their honor was held at noon. Miss Jessie Wilson, daughter of the President, was one of the most charming and democratic delegates in this party. From West Point to New Paltz by train, and thence by bus to Lake Mohonk they went, arriving in the early afternoon.

That night, the Conference was formally opened by the President, the Rev. I. Ibuki, of Japan, in an address that could scarcely be forgotten, and then Dr. John R. Mott, the Executive Secretary of the Federation, in his direct and powerful way, stated his desire that those present be ushered by God into some wondrous experience, relating them more closely to one another and to the expanding plans of His Kingdom.

The colored American delegates were Dr. John Hope, then President of Morehouse College; Dr. R. R. Moton, then Commandant at Hampton Institute; Dr. J. E. W. Kwegyir Aggrey, a native of West Africa, but representing Livingstone College, where he held a professorship; Mr. Channing H. Tobias, of the

Student Department of the Y.M.C.A.; and Mr. David Jones. Also present, representing the Y.W.C.A., were Miss Sadie Meriwether, of Howard University; Miss Carrie Bond, of Atlanta University; and Miss Josephine Pinyon and myself, representing the National Board of the Y.W.C.A. There was also a male quartet from Atlanta University that presented the only special music of the Conference. It is significant that all of this delegation became deeply interested in the Association movement and that Dr. Moton and Dr. Hope later became honored members of the National Council of the Young Men's Christian Associations.

Mr. Hunton, as leader of this delegation, was alert to its needs and to its actual participation. It was interesting to note his very quiet but intense enthusiasm, his unselfish and gentle yet positive guidance, and the deep respect, even devotion, he had won, not only from his American colleagues but from many present whom he had met six years before in the Far East. We all loved him very much, and the large, well-appointed hotel suite that had been selected for Mr. Hunton and me became a center for our delegation. There we rested, played, reasoned, and prayed together. He instilled in us the conviction that we had not yet tapped the fountain of our Christian resources and led us to an earnest seeking for it.

For Mr. Hunton and me personally it was one of the happiest weeks of our long married life. Absolutely free from the cares of the outer world, we had a closer companionship, a more perfect communion of spirit and ability to plan, than at any previous time. It was an ideal experience.

In a report of this Conference, one writer has said:

> Seven words suggest the salient characteristics of the Tenth Annual Conference of the World Student Christian Federation: environment, preparedness, accomplishment, fellowship, opportunity, strategy, and power.

Only a few added words are necessary relative to the environment. It was a kind of earthly paradise far removed from the harsh and ugly elements of life, and it was possible to feel there something of the contingency of human perfection. Mr. Hunton often iterated, "It is very easy to be good here."

It was very obvious that thorough preparation had preceded the Conference. Every detail had been worked out so that nothing could disturb the fundamental purposes of the gathering. Those who had come from many parts of the world to be participants had been making both consciously and unconsciously a spiritual advance toward it in the program they had been following in the preceding months. The accomplishments were attested to by the number and quality of both delegates and patrons, and the great diversity of nationalities that constituted the Conference. There, African and Nordic, Japanese and Chinese, Turk and Russian had joined heart and hands in one common purpose—the evangelization of the world. It was probably difficult for the Australian, the Boer from South Africa, and the lovely girl from Virginia, closely chaperoned by her mother and aunt, to comprehend immediately all that was involved in the pledge to help in the expansion of Christ's Kingdom here on earth. To keep their pledge, they must cast from them inherited customs and traditions, but they bravely did that and also bravely surmounted any that would have kept them from a full and free participation.

At this Conference the seating in the dining room had been so planned that acquaintance and fellowship would be assured. Each table seated from eight to ten persons and was numbered. Between meals these numbers were mixed and each person drew one as he entered the dining room and went to the table designated by his number. Each table had a permanent host and hostess, and Mr. Hunton and I were privileged to preside together. After dinner the first night, in summing up our guests, we counted one secretary and one student from the South, two Chinese, one Japanese, and a secretary of the International staff. We left our table just once—to dine at the special table of Dr. and Mrs. Mott —and I can recall no meals at which manners or conversations were less strained.

But it was in the sessions of the Conference itself that one sensed most deeply the abiding spirit of brotherhood, which ran like a golden thread through all the proceedings. Listening to Mr. F. S. Brockman and Mr. David Yui one morning tell of the stupendous problems Christian students were facing in China, and to Madame Orgewsky of Russia speaking another morning along the same line, one found oneself profoundly stirred—no matter how far removed by race and custom—and with a great longing for a deeper sense of purity and humility and for more spiritual power. Mr. Hunton and I confessed to each other after these sessions that we had freely but secretly shed tears. I remember saying to him that I did not know that I could love a Chinese so much, and I remember hearing one Japanese say to another at the close of the last session, after Mr. Hunton had spoken with such sincerity and depth of feeling on the Negro race, "I admire the Negro more than I have ever thought possible."

Men like Dr. Robert E. Speer, the Right Reverend Charles Brent, then Bishop of the Episcopal Diocese in the Philippines, Professor Cairns, and Dr. Isaac of India in stirring and wonderful addresses gave the Conference a clear vision of the world-wide opportunities of the Federation.

That a remarkable power and keen discernment dominated the meetings was manifest from beginning to end. One was ever conscious of a force direct, vital, and abundant that kept the purpose of the meeting always the foremost thing in the minds of the delegates.

It was at the closing meeting that Mr. Hunton made the last great public appeal of his life. His address had been prepared for the Tokyo Conference after two years of research and thoughtful writing. He had also worked rather carefully over his address for the Lake Mohonk Meeting, but he spent, too, more hours of preparation in prayerful meditation than I had ever known him to do before. He stirred very deeply the hearts of his hearers, who had come from all parts of the world. It was his last appeal for the *all-inclusive* brotherhood of man and it was a masterful one. It is one of the few addresses of the Conference printed in its entirety in the report that followed later, and because it is there given in full, I shall reprint here only an excerpt from the opening and the closing of his appealing challenge. He began by saying:

As we address ourselves to the topic for this hour, our minds turn irresistibly to two events which are being appropriately and impressively commemorated this year—events that are of particular interest to the Negro race and stand among the most inspiring that have influenced the progress of man. This is the fiftieth anniversary of the abolition of slavery in this country under the presidency of Abraham Lincoln. It is also the centennial anniversary of David Livingstone, by whom a path was blazed through the heart of Africa, marked with the sign of the cross and also by a call sent forth summoning Christendom to the tremendous task of healing the "open sore" of the world.

It is very fitting therefore that this conference, representing the Christian students of the world, should pause to receive new inspiration from the heroic deeds of Livingstone and Lincoln and to rededicate ourselves to the principles for which both laid down their lives.

Then in conclusion he exclaimed:

Pray with us that there shall come to the heart of the world not only an intellectual interpretation of the brotherhood of man, but a spiritual acceptance of it, so that speedily there may dawn a glorious morning when man shall not judge his fellow-man by color, race, tradition or any of the accidents of life but by righteousness and truth and unselfish service to humanity.

After the profound but very vibrant silence that followed Mr. Hunton's address, Mr. Mott in his inimitable manner made the closing address, speaking with such eloquence, insistency, and compelling power that the delegates came to their feet in re-affirmation of their allegiance to the World Student Christian Federation and in a final united prayer for strength and consecration needed for successful service.

CHAPTER NINE

Devotional Life

A N Y BIOGRAPHICAL sketch of William A. Hunton, however brief it might be, that failed to make special note of his devotional life would omit the most salient characteristic and expression of the whole man.

James Truslow Adams has written:

> Perhaps it would be a good idea, as fantastic as it sounds, to muffle every telephone, stop every motor and halt all activity for an hour some day to give people a chance to ponder for a few minutes on what it is all about and why they are living and what they really want.

Such a respite from the hum and grind of existence would no doubt prove a wonderful life-giving tonic to most folks. However, for the subject of this book it would not have been necessary to prescribe such a period of silence. As his nephew, the Reverend Louis Hunton Berry, once remarked: "He was skilled in the rare art of conversing with himself." Not only within the confines of his own comfortable study, but in the center of office activity, or if dropped in some seemingly God-forsaken spot while traveling, he could retire within himself and commune with his own soul and with God.

As a mere youth, Mr. Hunton exhibited an unusual zeal in Christian service. His father and his sister Victoria, both devoted Christians, encouraged and helped him, while his lifelong spiritual mentor, the Rev. J. Albert Johnson, greatly influenced his religious attitudes. His brothers and pals were vaguely aware that life held something different for him, even though he entered heartily into their common life together and casually took and gave the persiflage usual among youth. They respected that quality in him that somehow set him apart from them.

During the period when he was but a growing youth, through

his short career as a school teacher, and during the three years spent in very active service in the church and the Young Men's Christian Association at Ottawa, Mr. Hunton was advancing into a more and more intimate relationship with God, until, in that future to which he was also rapidly moving, neither hardship nor success, neither skepticism nor strange tenets, would be able to shake the fundamental religious principles of his life.

The dominant note of his life was to know the will of Him whom he would try to follow, and this desire led him into a fixed habit of worship—the habit of acknowledging shortcomings; of offering prayers for forgiveness of sins; and of finding joy in new visions and inspirations.

This habit of worship was strengthened rather than diminished when he found his place of service in the Young Men's Christian Association. He wrote from his first conference with the other secretaries, after joining the staff of the International Committee:

> Sixteen of the International Secretaries were in prayerful conference from ten o'clock this morning until three this afternoon.

And then from a secretarial conference at Hartford, Connecticut, he wrote again, May, 1895:

> The three hours' session this morning was a most blessed waiting on God with intense heart searchings. There are nearly three hundred secretaries in attendance. There were about seven hundred delegates in all at the Convention.

Writing from still another secretarial convention, he exclaimed:

> Yesterday was a day of great heart-searching with me and I did not write you. I thank the Lord for my experience and believe and hope that it was only the beginning of deeper searchings to follow. I have been wonderfully helped in my spiritual life. I was up at six this morning and had my Bible study of nearly forty-five minutes before breakfast.

I was wedded to Mr. Hunton with no delusions relative to his loyalties, for he had been very painstaking in explaining to me that he had pledged his supreme devotion to his Lord and that his

122

work must retain his first consideration. Also, very early in my married life, I came to know that there were times when Mr. Hunton desired to be wholly alone. It was a desire that was very deep with him now and then. I think it was a real yearning for a silence in which he might find new convictions and new strength to bulwark against spiritual weakness. It was perhaps an effort to find that inner chamber of the soul, where, as Dr. Rauschenbusch has said:

> In a moment, in the turning of a thought,
>   I am where God is.
> Big things become small and small things become great,
>   The near becomes far and the far becomes near.

The Northfield conferences that Mr. Hunton found a great happiness in attending, throughout his life, were at all times a "Mountain Top" experience for him. From his first summer there, before we were married, until near the end of his life he would write in an exalted strain of his experiences.

He exclaimed, just before going to a conference:

> I am rather glad of the days that I am to spend quietly at Northfield. I need the spiritual strengthening that the environment there and the time to meditate will afford. I am in no sense what I ought to be and what it is possible for me to be.

And after his arrival there, he wrote:

> I received a great blessing this morning as Mr. Moody spoke on the Holy Spirit. I realized his coming into my life as I surrendered myself wholly to Jesus Christ. I came home singing in my heart:
>
> > O! to be nothing, nothing—
> >   Only to lie at his feet
> > A broken and emptied vessel
> >   For the Master's use made meet.

In July, 1900, he said after a session that had deeply moved him:

> The main conference is over. Six hundred students in attendance—the largest yet held. Yesterday was a great day in the Lord. I have received great blessing and many valuable suggestions. I have decided to submit prayerfully all of my planning, as well as all my doing, to the Lord for his guid-

ance as never before. I am conscious of shortcomings in this and of consequent weakness and unfruitfulness. It is so easy to fall into the habit of trying to run things myself. And then this resolution will cut into some of my indulgences. Pray for me, dear, that I may please Him in all things, cost what it may.

Then, during a still later conference:

At last I have finished reading President King's "Rational Living." I seem to read so slowly; yet I hope that I have absorbed a good deal of useful information from this great book—information I mean, that will bear fruit in my own life.

Dr. Speer gave us a fine address this morning on John the Baptist—a man with a mission from God. But I have been helped most by an address by Dr. Fosdick on the Reinstatement of Peter into our Lord's service. For two years or more, I have not been living up to the best that is possible for' me—I have gotten away from the path of my great life mission. With God's forgiveness and by His grace, I return and shall strive to live up to the best that is possible for me in every way.

Reading while traveling made fruitful many hours that would otherwise have proven very tedious. His books were chosen with great discrimination, and although those on religious topics outnumbered all others, he enjoyed history, biography, and fiction very much. But whatever other books he had in his valise, there was always room left for his Bible and one book of a devotional nature. Typical of his reading habit is the following statement:

I have nearly finished that book that I have carried about so long, "Many Infallible Proofs." I want you to read it. In fact I believe in this day of scepticism and doubt we should read a book like it at least once a year. I am enjoying it ever so much.

But it was really his Bible that meant most to him. It was helpful to him in the solution of all his problems, in all that he wanted to know and wanted to accomplish. He was irked somewhat whenever his environment proved unfavorable to the fullest possible use of it. In the hundreds of letters that he penned me during a quarter of a century, no other subject save that of the devotion between us took so much space. He would write about his own discoveries and the discoveries of others in the Scripture; he would

124

commend special passages for my consideration and as a balance to support me in our absence from each other. In his shining moments, he would write with a deep intensity of his proud fiery belief in the word of God. Though he was never domineering nor argumentative, yet there was deep poignance in his plea to young men for more ardor and more faithfulness in the use of the Bible.

When we were separated from each other on the first day of the year in 1900, he sent me the following message:

> I have prayed that God will wipe out all my past sins which are so many, and that he will keep me henceforth from all sin. I have selected for my text for the year, John 8: 29, I like the "Revised Version" better—"He that sent me is with me. He hath not left me alone, for I do always the things that are pleasing to Him." That ought to keep me pure and sweet and fruitful of good all the year. Pray that I may live up to it every moment.

Before mailing the above, he added the lines below:

> While meditating I was moved to select another passage for this year's text—John 14: 21: "He that hath my commandments and keepeth them, he it is that loveth me; and he that loveth me shall be loved of my Father, and I will love him and will manifest myself unto him." I want to know more about the love of Jesus, to drink deeper of it. I will therefore, by his grace, study his word daily, prayerfully, that I may know his commandments and constantly look to Him for strength to keep them. May this wonderful blessing be yours also this year. Pray for me.

Anent this subject, he wrote again:

> Spent an hour and a half with my Bible. So many times it is not convenient for me to have my daily Bible study, and then I suffer the loss of power—power to control myself and power with others. The Lord blesses me greatly beyond what I deserve. I am always conscious of the fact that if I would spend more time with Him, I would have more power with men.

And still later:

> I have resumed my morning Bible studies during the last

few days, and I wonder that I ever can allow anything to prevent my devoting at least half an hour every morning to such profitable exercise. Surely there is something wrong when we are too busy to feed the soul. I fear that I am criminally neglectful also in respect to study. I could do so much more effective work if I should study more. Can you help me?

Mr. Hunton was really systematic in his study, work, and rest as far as his schedule of almost constant travel would permit, but he was also very critical of himself and very often would turn on a very searching light for self-analysis.

He very rarely used manuscript in delivering his addresses, but made very careful outlines, meditated upon them deeply and sought to make any position he took tenable. He realized the importance of thorough preparation. I have known him to sit for hours with note-book, pencil, and Bible, making ready for a young men's Bible study class that would probably last but a half hour. I have read over many of his outlines and they show much painstaking study. Just after making ready to conduct a Bible class at Howard University on one of his visits with the Association there, he wrote the following lines so typical of his constant humility:

I have spent nearly a half hour thinking on my outline. I wish I could tell you what I have thought, and better still, I wish I could live the life I have seen mirrored in my meditations. Is it wrong to tell others to do what one has not done one's self?

In his own private life Mr. Hunton was called upon very early and on down through the years to face many crises that of necessity brought reaction in his spiritual life. Two years before our marriage, he had lost that venerable and revered father who had meant so much in his life, and very soon after our lives had been united came the death of two stalwart brothers, Robert, a lawyer in the Northwest, and Augustus, a business man in Canada, both rather young for the Reaper. Then followed the death of our first-born, lovely little Bernice, and then three years later of our first son, our first William Alphaeus. Death stalked us for several years, Mr. Hunton losing still another brother, Stanton, who died in the far Northwest, and other relatives. And then I lost father, sister, and aunt in rather rapid succession. All of these had gained a very warm devotion from Mr. Hunton.

His grief was very human and deep but never tinged with despair. He had a very firmly founded faith and courage that both, fortified his own spirit and gave him, strength to hold me from utter hopelessness. Although heartbroken himself when he had to leave for a conference immediately after the death of our little boy, he could send me these unforgotten lines:

> Lo, eyes were made for the light
> And souls were made for joy.
> But eyes must be blinded by night,
> And souls must be burdened by grief.
> That alike they may find relief,
> Relief from the strain of the light
> And strength from the strain of joy.

And then after my father's death:

> But not today. Then be content poor heart;
>   God's plans, like lilies pure and white, unfold.
> We must not tear the close-shut leaves apart;
>   Time will reveal the chalices of gold.
> And if by patient toil, we reach the land
>   Where tired feet with sandals loose may rest,
> When we shall clearly know and understand,
>   I think that we shall say that God knew best.

I wish to paint no halo about the head of my husband nor convey the slightest idea that he held any blind idealism; nor could I endure any overdrawn picture of his religious life, for I loved the very human in him as well as the divine. But I think that all of those who ever touched Mr. Hunton had an awareness of his sincere and abundant Christian life. In a fuller measure than is granted many, he held very precious the teachings of Jesus and essayed to emulate them in his own life. He was simply one of the faithful ones who never doubted the blessedness and effectiveness of the mission of our Lord, who stood revealed to him as a wonderful personality.

When he returned from Japan, he brought home a copy of the precepts of Iyeyasu, translated by Professor K. Wadagaki, as follows:

Life is like unto a long journey with a heavy load. Let thy steps be slow and steady, that thou stumble not.

Persuade thyself that imperfection and inconvenience is the natural lot of mortals, and there will be no room for discontent, neither for despair. When ambitious desires arise in thy heart, recall the days of extremity thou hast passed through.

Forbearance is the root of quietness and assurance forever. Look upon wrath as thine enemy. If thou knowest only what it is to conquer, and knowest not what it is to be defeated, woe unto thee! It will fare ill with thee. Find fault with thyself rather than with others. Better the less than the more.

These precepts he wrote in his note-book, often read them, and, when I was impatient at times, would quote them quite as freely as he did his Bible.

The most real thing in his whole life, public or private, was his high Christian standard. This was the mainspring in all his labors and in all his achievements. This it was, founded upon strong religious beliefs, that prevented doubt from ever mastering him; he had no time nor reason to become self-centered; he was always humble and could meet all crises with a quiet poise.

He wrote toward the end of his career:

Yes, my work is very heavy. There is many a twist and hard knot. There are many unfortunate conditions to be met and many difficult problems to be solved, but it is no time for flinching—I must go on. I am deeply thankful that I am conscious of my Father's help and your constant care and inspiration.

In planning for the Young People's Christian Congress held in Atlanta, Georgia, April, 1914, under the leadership of Dr. John R. Mott, a change of the place of the conference first decided upon, led to some unexpected difficulties which necessitated a conference of those who were promoting the gathering. The student secretaries of the Colored Men's Department of the Young Men's Christian Association and Miss Josephine Pinyon and I, representing the National Board of the Young Women's Christian Association, met in the home of Dr. John Hope, then President of Morehouse College. It was a difficult moment, for we were all

128

feeling rather deeply and were no doubt impatient. Although Mr. Hunton was stirred too, he sat perfectly calm and cool as we urged him to take the immediate and positive action that we believed the situation required. His deliberateness made us even more insistent until Dr. Hope reminded us that Mr. Hunton would act with precision when we were really ready for it. He did act with a courage and directness that cleared away all the difficulties and dangers that we had faced, and the Congress was a great success. However, conflicts and controversies for any purpose were always hard for him and hurt him physically as well as spiritually. It was no doubt the strain involved in effecting the success of this Congress that brought about the sudden collapse that he suffered at that time. Yet his observations and experiences with his fellows, however unhappy they might be, left no trace of bitterness. Instead, they intensified his love and his desire to serve. He had set his sails early in life and across the far horizon was able to vision a better dawn. Christ was his pilot; his Bible his chart. He could endure storms, for he would keep on a charted sea.

Mr. Hunton's human devotion was so closely allied to his whole devotional life that it is difficult to think of them apart.

His love was an integral part of his being and very sacred and always to the forefront in his prayers. He loved his family profoundly to the end and prayed very constantly for their well-being. His home-coming was always a very precious event for all of us, looked forward to and planned for with a sense of joy and devotion.

From the London Jubilee, in 1894, at the time of our first wedding anniversary, he had written:

> Our love shall flow on like a river—ever onward over rocks and shoals of trying experience; by fields of heavy hanging grain, the fruit of successful toil; under the clouds, under the sunshine it will flow onward. A great river of love it is that will take us at last into the haven of eternal rest.

All through the years it was the same, and in July, 1913, nineteen years after that first anniversary, he wrote:

> On this anniversary I wish to renew my pledge of devotion to you and to thank God for the great love that binds us se-

curely together. I shall ever try to be strong and courageous
for your dear sake. My heart is with you and the children.

Mr. Hunton's life has been a sublime benediction not only to
the lives of his many close associates but to hundreds who knew
him in those years when he believed worship to be a necessary and
permanent privilege of the human spirit, and in that belief he was
tested, took those first steps, saw horizons widen, and reached those
richer culminating years.

CHAPTER TEN

Shadowed By Illness

WHEN Mr. Hunton was stricken in 1914 by what was to prove a fatal illness, fully twenty-six years of his life had been devoted to the development of Association work in the United States among colored men. This was a little more than half of the sum total of all the years of his life. He had in a quarter of a century broken down barriers of insularity and passivity, swept aside recalcitrant opinions and efforts, converted impotence and insouciance into vigor and interest, and thereby blazed a trail into the sure light of understanding and co-operation. With the help of his associates, he had made so firm the groundwork of this new empire of the soul that he had been able not only to vision but to achieve.

However, those twenty-six years of pioneering and divine inspiration were full of arduous and exhausting work and responsibility. When one adds together the days of all these years that were spent, for the most part, traveling over the South under conditions unfavorable to both body and spirit, and remembers the poor and scant food and fare with which oftener than otherwise he had to be content, when one realizes that he must have experienced at times great yearning for the companionship at home and the nursery hours of his children, where he could find relief from problems and cares, the wonder is not that he finished with this life so early, but rather that he was able to carry on so long.

In 1904 he made a trip through the Gulf States that lasted well into the spring and that proved rather too much for his tired body. He returned to our Atlanta home with his system charged with malaria. His heart weakened under the strain and he was desperately ill for some time. However, a summer with his relatives in the more bracing atmosphere of Michigan and Ontario gave him back strength and a measure of health, and he was at work again in the autumn. Calmness was a very marked trait of his character that helped him greatly at the time of any crisis, either of body or mind, and it made recovery less difficult. As I traveled with him north that summer, one noting his deep regard for my comfort would have thought that I rather than he was the invalid. His letters, written daily after I had returned to our children, while expressing thankfulness for comforts and for God's presence near him, also were bright with good cheer and the quiet rich humor for which he was noted. He wrote:

> I fear that I shall have to ask for a raise at the office this fall to buy an entirely new outfit unless you can help me out. What with so much coddling, massaging and nourishing food, I shall not be able to wear these clothes unless you know how to put in some gussets or something of the kind. I am really afraid to weigh again. But the truth is that I am just a fakir for I don't feel sick at all.

The following winter saw him as active as ever. The next spring and early summer he made very positive efforts to raise the salary of a first student secretary for his department and was very happy in his success.

On his birthday in 1905, he expressed himself thus:

> I turn another mile post in my life today. I feel young, healthy, strong and hopeful—very thankful for all that God has done for me. I have strong faith in our future and desire to make it the best part of our life. Forty-two years have gone by. I can hardly hope for as many more—certainly not so many years of active service. So that I am anxious that not a year of my future be misspent. Do I say a year? My! what a spendthrift I am. The days and hours should and must be counted as golden.

One of the most tragic incidents of our married life was the Atlanta riot in the fall of 1906.

When, in 1898, Mr. Hunton was joined in his activities by Mr. Moorland, he selected Atlanta as the best place for our home, because it was a very desirable center for the supervision of student work to which he then hoped to devote the major part of his time.

We had barely reached Atlanta, in the spring of 1899, when the quiet of a Sabbath day was shattered by the news of the lynch-

132

ing of a Negro, Sam Hose by name, accused of the usual crime. This happened in a town nearby, and was made the more ghastly by the burning of the victim and the distribution of parts of his body for souvenirs. In consternation my husband and I drew apart from our friends to consider what to do. The wisdom of having our expected child born to us in such an environment seemed quite doubtful, but after prayer and deep thought, we decided to remain.

We put much joyous enthusiasm into the building of our modest but precious home. Eunice came and bound our love more closely, and later our second Alphaeus took the place of the first, whom we had lost.

But after eight contented years in Atlanta, the pent-up hate and envy of a dominant group broke upon us suddenly, though not without some previous rumblings. In a moment all our sense of security was gone, and we had to realize that we, as colored people, had really no rights as citizens whatsoever. It left us very empty, for we knew in that hour that all for which we had labored and sacrificed belonged not to us but to a ruthless mob.

Mr. Hunton, who was at home at the time of the riot, suffered a stunning blow to his fine sensitive soul as well as to his physical condition. He had a severe attack of colitis, to which he had become quite susceptible after his illness two years before. His spirit lost for the first time its resilience, and he kept grimly serious. Preparations for his trip to the Orient were being made, but he now felt very positively that he could not go so far and leave his family amid the scenes of that late riot. His frequent necessary absences from his family immediately after this trouble filled him with so much anxiety that he was hardly able to go on with his work. Therefore, in December, 1906, we closed our home and went north to remain during the months that Mr. Hunton would be abroad. We did not then realize that we were taking final leave.

Although the deep tragedy of Atlanta grew less poignant with Mr. Hunton's visit to Far Eastern countries the next year, he never quite escaped its physical reaction, and it no doubt contributed toward his final collapse. However, during 1909 and the first half of 1910, he felt again very strong and vigorous and, for a time,

133

carried forward not only his own work but that of Mr. Moorland, who had also been subject to a physical collapse.

Through 1909 and 1910 I was in Europe with our children, but there was little interruption in the frequency and intimacy of the correspondence between Mr. Hunton and me that had always been sustaining and precious. We felt very close together, despite the ocean between, and his letters teemed with interest as he so graphically pictured the crowded events of that period of high achievement. He was boyishly joyous in the progress being made in his department. Yet the disturbing thought persisted in my mind that he might be overworking, and this thought did bring me back home before I had fully finished the studies I had undertaken.

It was in the fall of 1910 that his throat began to show signs of weakness, and, in spite of two minor operations that winter, he never could afterwards overcome a chronic coughing. Although he went forward with the full schedule before him through 1911 and 1912 with his usual spontaneity and interest, in 1913 he began to show positive signs of physical weakness, and the following summer we went to a very quiet and private spot on Long Island in order that he could have absolute rest. His spirit was not quite so tranquil as was usual with him. Difficult problems had arisen in his field, and he felt that it was absolutely necessary for the good of the work that they be solved at the International Secretaries Conference that would be held in September. But we fished, loafed, and read, and with the fall he was refreshed and calm.

Again he traveled constantly and widely, although he was finding himself absolutely compelled to stop and rest here and there in the midst of his work. At times I wrote almost frantically, pleading with him to give up and come home for care and rest, but he felt the urgency of his work too much to take heed.

The frequent changes of climate that his travel schedule required were very detrimental to his health at that time, and he was often in the throes of grippe. Writing from Washington, D. C., after visiting a school in October, 1913, he said:

Caught more cold by sleeping on a cot in a very cold room.

134

I shall go to bed very early to-night and also take some medicine.

Just a little later he wrote from Atlanta, Ga., the following:

> The secret fact is that I have not been well since I came from Columbus. I stayed in all day Sunday after taking some medicine. Monday and Tuesday I had a stenographer in and only gave her some letters and a few other things. But yesterday my heart's action was very sluggish and I went uptown with difficulty. So I turned in and here I am. Thought last night that I would have to send for you. I then wondered what you would do about the children—for I knew that you would come pell-mell.
>
> Now don't worry, dear, I am not suffering a bit. Am only tired. I would be much happier if you were here to talk with me and to make me stay in bed, etc., but I would rather that you would not come now. Dr. Jones was here this morning and says that I need rest, that I may sit up to-morrow, go to the Y.M.C.A. Saturday and not leave town until next week.
>
> I slept some last night and have been sleeping and eating well to-day. My work here is all arranged so there is nothing to bother me. So do not think of coming to Atlanta now. I will certainly let you know if I need you. Of course your presence would cheer me. But I will be up before you could get started—in fact, before you get this letter.

We had been expecting Mr. Hunton to spend Thanksgiving with us. He had been absent from home for many weeks. The children were dancing in the joy of their anticipation, and the turkey and plum pudding were both brown before his telegram arrived telling us that he could not reach us. I suspected the truth at once. He was really too sick to continue his travel from the far South.

We now began to look forward to Christmas. He would surely be coming to us then.

By December Mr. Hunton was filling engagements in some of the larger colleges and universities of the Middle West. While en route to the University of Michigan, he was compelled by illness to linger in the home of his sister Victoria in Detroit. She wrote me at that time that he needed rest badly and that I should make him take it.

He had promised us that he would arrive in time for a visit

to Santa Claus and then spend a whole glorious week with us. He came even earlier than we had anticipated, but it was evident at a glance that he was very spent and needed much rest and care.

All our holiday activity was restrained. Mr. Hunton left the house only twice—once for a trip to his office. He expressed the desire to make a few visits just before the New Year, and we made a list of Brooklyn friends on whom we would call. We did reach the home of Dr. and Mrs. Owen Waller, but when we left there, he asked, with an apology, if I would mind returning home, as he did not feel equal to seeing anyone else.

A staff meeting in Washington for the Colored Men's Department had been planned for the first of January, 1914, and Mr. Hunton made sleeping car reservation and packed his bags, but, at the last moment, was too ill to make the trip. It was the first time that he had been absent from such a meeting. Still, he again made a brave effort to recover his physical strength and kept cheerful and humorous, although he knew that he must soon rest. He had long wanted me to go with him to Ottawa and through beautiful northeastern Canada, and so he kept saying, "Wait.till summer, we will take our second honeymoon and you can be the boss."

In February, 1914, Dr. Mott summoned a group of Young Men's and Young Women's Christian Association people to meet at his office and revealed his ideas for a Negro student congress that should be held in the South the coming spring. Some plans were formulated, and Mr. Hunton was charged with the first responsibility of preparation for the congress. He was really ill then, but began planning with the thoroughness and earnestness so characteristic of him as he realized in it a great opportunity for the mobilization of the choice youth in our schools for Christian service. He seemed for a time to be re-invigorated for the task. However, the difficulties involved in arranging for the Congress at Atlanta, Georgia, to which I have already referred, proved too great a strain for him. While waiting at the Association building there for an answer to an important telegram he had sent, he collapsed completely. Our old family physician, Dr. Jones, was called, and when Mr. Hunton had been sufficiently strengthened,

136

he was taken to the home of Professor J. B. Watson, whose guests we were at the time. With us were President Hope, Miss Josephine Pinyon, members of his own staff, and Richard B. Harrison, one of his old Canadian pals. All of us realized that Mr. Hunton was a very ill man, but I think that not one of us suspected that it was but the beginning of the end, and least of all did Mr. Hunton himself suspect it.

Remaining with him until he was able to move about again, I returned to our children in Brooklyn. In the meantime, President Hope, who was also feeling the need of rest, planned to go with Mr. Hunton to Hot Springs, Arkansas. Mr. Hunton wrote himself at that time:

> I lay down most of yesterday morning and afternoon and realize that I am gaining strength. We expect to hear from Hot Springs to-morrow, and I shall go somewhere for rest if not there. Am writing Mr. Shipp to that effect.

Mr. Shipp was the Office Secretary of the International Committee.

Fortunately perhaps, because of a large fire there, it was not possible to reserve accommodations at Hot Springs, and plans were then made to spend a week or two at Atlantic City, after which he would rest in Washington for a while. We were purchasing a house there, and in it he and his nephew, Benjamin Hunton, a student at Howard University, kept "bachelors' quarters." This was very convenient for Mr. Hunton, as the headquarters of the Colored Men's Department of the Association was then in Washington. But when I met him in Philadelphia, prepared to go with him to Atlantic City, although only ten days had elapsed since I had left him in Atlanta, I was shocked by his appearance and so filled with an alarming certitude of the seriousness of his illness that, without revealing my real fears, I begged and finally persuaded him to go first to Washington for expert medical advice.

Mr. Hunton was still much engrossed in the forthcoming Student Congress and wanted to keep at work on it by using his secretary at home. However, my veto, strengthened by that of Mr. Moorland, quickly terminated that plan.

Then there came that never to be forgotten Saturday afternoon in April with its unexpected and tragic revelation when we were alone in the house. Settled in a comfortable chair by his bedroom window, Mr. Hunton was reading. I had gone to prepare some nourishment for him. Suddenly there was a strange call from him that took me quickly to his side. He was having a hemorrhage from the lungs.

After a thorough examination, Dr. A. M. Curtis, our friend as well as physician, tried to adjust us as calmly as possible to the truth of Mr. Hunton's condition, which he himself now realized. But again he quickly rallied, and when I returned from a hurried trip to see our children, who were in Brooklyn, he was almost gay in spirits and could warn me against leaving him in the hands of such lovely ladies as the nurse and my good friend, now Mrs. Bauduit. However, within an hour another hemorrhage shook his frame and a battle for his life began, which lasted several weeks. Much of the time he lay in a restless unconsciousness.

It was at this period that the Negro Young People's Congress to which he had devoted his last energies convened at Atlanta. Telegrams poured in to him from that meeting, and prayers were again and again offered for him there. Dr. Mott stopped in the midst of those busy days to send us appreciative and affectionate messages. But Mr. Hunton was not able to know of these evidences of esteem until weeks later. David Jones wrote at that time:

> I am sure that Dean (referring to Mr. Moorland) has visited you and has told you about the Atlanta Congress. If we ever missed a person we surely missed you, for as John Hope told us "There are none of you fellows that can scrap and keep your temper like Hunton."
>
> While you were absent from the Congress in person it was inspiring to see the number of men there whose lives you had touched and brought into the active work. Among them were Tobias, Trent, Aggrey and scores of others along with myself, and we were there simply because you took an interest in us and led us on. How sincerely do we all hope that in some small way our lives may be as fruitful as yours.
>
> The Congress was a great success, but it was a success because for so many years you had put your life in work for the students of our colleges.
>
> I will not burden you with a long letter. I just want to

138

say that every day I pray that God may give you back your strength and your old time vigor, for we need you more than you can appreciate.

But Mr. Hunton again fought his way back from the very edge of life; he refused to believe that it was a losing fight even though a noted specialist had given his opinion that he could scarcely last three weeks. His brother George came from Montreal, his sister Victoria from Detroit, and his younger sister, Mary, from her home in St. Louis. One day when the nurse had left the room for a moment, he beckoned me to his side and, though very weak, firmly grasped my hand and whispered: "We are pals, dear, and I can win with you close by me." It was often necessary in those trying days for me to find privacy to fight my emotions and to gain strength to match my faith with that of my husband or appear at least to do so. Everywhere there was great anxiety as he made his brave effort. Letters and telegrams came from individuals, student and city Associations, and many other organizations in every part of the country. But the nurse kept him quiet, and the cares of the outer world as well as its joys receded. At that time Dr. Mott, who had kept in close touch with the family, wrote:

> Dear Hunton, I am rejoiced to know that you are steadily improving. I counsel you to take no chances. Do not over-exert yourself. Make all conditions as favorable as possible for a complete recovery. You were never needed as much as in these years.

Mr. L. Wilbur Messer, General Secretary of the Chicago Associations and a good friend of Mr. Hunton for many years, sent the following letter:

> My Dear Friend Hunton:
>
> On returning home from our world tour, both Mrs. Messer and myself are deeply pained to learn of your illness and of your temporary retirement from your Association duties. Your well-rounded Christian life and efficient service for young men have won for you not only the confidence but the personal affection of many who have known you through these long years of faithful labor. These friends will remember you now in the days of your weakness with the earnest prayer that God

will give you a large measure of His grace and an abiding peace in these hours of meditation.

It must be gratifying to you to note the great advance which has been made in the department to which you have given your life. Our Heavenly Father is very good in letting us see here some of the results of faithful seed sowing in His name, but the real reward is reserved for our eternal joy.

Our tour in the non-Christian lands has been one of deep significance and we return with an increased confidence in the power of our Association movement and in its adaptability to serve all races and all conditions of men.

Please remember me as one of your abiding and appreciative friends.

I hope to hear, as in the letter just received from Mr. Moorland, that you are steadily improving in health and that you will soon be restored to your labor of love.

It was letters such as that, from many, many friends, that Mr. Hunton so gratefully and humbly read in late May of that year, when his condition had very definitely improved, and that strengthened his resolution to fight it out. When in early June, under the direction of the International Committee, Mr. Moorland and George Hunton went to Saranac Lake, New York, to seek an abode there for us, Mr. Hunton entered into the plans with a surprising enthusiasm.

Dr. Edward L. Parks, then Registrar and Treasurer of Howard University, had sent this word:

My Dear Brother Hunton:

I have thought of you many times and remembered you in prayer during these weeks. How I should like to sit down beside you and talk about the great things of life and eternity. But I know that the Great Friend is with you through His spirit.

With cordial regards to yourself and wife in which Mrs. Parks joins.

The Great Friend was with him. For so many years he had relied upon God that it was but natural that he should now find in Him courage for the great trial that was upon him. The letter that touched his heart very deeply and that comforted him throughout his ordeal was that written by Mr. Richard C. Morse, General Secretary of the International Committee, under whom Mr.

140

Hunton had worked from the very beginning of his service. It said:

My Dear Friend:

On my return home it deeply pains me to hear of your illness, and I eagerly write to express to you my heartfelt brotherly sympathy. And my next and urgent thought—in token of this sympathy—is to join Mr. Marling and Mr. Shipp in urging upon you as your first obligation to all who love you best and who are most interested in the work you and they love is to *get well*.

In order to do this you must cultivate the patience of hope— the patience and the hope of those who walk not by sight but by faith.

Dr. Jowett says of those who refuse to walk by sight and walk by faith in our Lord that to such in every event, whether prosperous or adverse, God comes not only to be present but to commune with the believer and to make all things work together for his good. When you are sick and in need of the rest of faith in order to get well, then faith in our Father leads also to a restful faith in the disciples whom He sends to minister to you in His name.

I heartily congratulate you and Mrs. Hunton on the sort of fellow disciples He has sent you in the persons of the Committee and those of its staff who are in most intimate touch with you. Do not feel troubled or worried in confiding entirely in them. Such worry of mind interferes with that recovery for which we are all praying. Increase of faith and trust will give you an increase of that rest and peace that is the pathway to recovery. Along this path the work you have lived and wrought for is beckoning you. What you have been to it and in it is gratefully appreciated and entitles you to the rest you now need in the interest of the work itself. Mrs. Morse joins me in prayerful sympathy and in cordial greeting to both Mrs. Hunton and yourself.

Ever affectionately, your fellow secretary,

I still marvel at the tranquillity of Mr. Hunton's spirit at that time—a tranquillity that was deep and permanent and that carried with it the power to still our troubled souls also and give us brief periods, at least, of high courage and hope. If he seemed wistful and very tender at times, it was not for himself but for those whom he knew were suffering for him.

In early June he was well enough to be taken for brief drives. He enjoyed the more the beautiful suburbs of Washington because he had spent almost four months indoors. That city had always held advantages as a center for Association activity among colored men, and he had spent much time there from the very beginning of his service. Again and again after leaving Atlanta, we had been urged to make it our home, and had about decided to do so as soon as our children should begin their college life. But now, though he did not know it, these drives were giving him his last beautiful glimpses of a city he had grown to love.

By the end of June, Mr. Hunton was able to start for Saranac Lake. We rested en route over a day in Brooklyn with our very good friends, Mr. and Mrs. Harry Hairston, who have ever been the guardians of our children when it has been necessary for us to leave them. We were accompanied on this trip by another faithful friend who gave up all else to remain with us: Mrs. Emma Gray, now Mrs. William Bauduit. She had Mr. Hunton's sincere devotion and he greatly depended upon her during his entire illness for the loving care that she knew so well how to minister.

It was a precarious journey for one who had been as ill as Mr. Hunton, and we were filled with much anxiety and were prepared for any emergency during that very long night from New York City to Saranac Lake as we kept close watch over him while he slept.

Here again there was an unexpected token of the esteem in which Mr. Hunton was so widely held. Two young students from one of the southern schools were porters on our train and had seen him carried into a Pullman car. Though not in his car, they came quickly to speak to him and to offer themselves for any service. We did want some milk and they promised to get it for us. From somewhere along the road during the night they secured a fresh new pail of very good milk. The next morning, with others, they helped Mr. Hunton from the train at Saranac Lake and stood in silent homage for a moment, with caps in hand, before boarding the train to go on to Lake Placid.

We were met at the station by a Mr. Roberts, our lessor, who was to prove a very staunch friend during our stay there, and by a son of Mr. Hunton's brother George, who was also ill and who had come from Montreal to recuperate at Saranac Lake. At the lovely cottage that Mr. Moorland and George had secured for us, a trained nurse and a physician awaited us. We were in an entirely new world—there in the very deepest fastness of the lofty Adirondacks, far removed from the fever and fret of life—we were to have an extraordinary experience in making a determined fight for the annihilation of one of the most formidable enemies of man—tuberculosis. The place chosen for the conflict gave us every advantage, but well for our hope and our courage that we did not know at the moment that the battle there would last so long—for almost a year and a half.

CHAPTER ELEVEN

At Saranac Lake

THE LITTLE village of Saranac Lake, with its population in 1914 of a scant five thousand, one-fourth of whom were seeking for health, is situated in the very heart of the Adirondack region. It offers not only a serene environment and a perfect climate of exceptional healing qualities to those affected with any form of phthisis, but the sheer loveliness of the scenery imparts to those in good health a new exuberance and elation of spirit that cannot be denied.

We reached the village in the early summer, at the floodtime of its beauty, and were even in our first hours there overpowered by it. Mr. Hunton had been quickly placed in his bed on a sleeping porch that gave him a wide panoramic view of long mountain ranges with their peaks towering to meet the sky, many of them still snow-crested. The soothing sound of purling waters between creviced rock could cut across space to our ears, and wide reaches of woods, dressed in their soft colorings of summer green, stretched in vain up toward the peaks. After a period of silence in which no doubt there was devotion, Mr. Hunton turned to me and in hushed voice exclaimed: "Any man, dear, should be able to get well here."

This was just the beginning of those weeks and months when hour after hour he drank in not only the life-giving air of that region but the superb soul-filling glory of its scenery. He had been told by all of his friends that he must lead a pleasant, idle languid existence at Saranac. Good Doctor Kinghorn saw to it that he should not be led into any temptation to exercise by keeping him absolutely on his back for many months. And yet I think that there was never a time in his whole life when his mind was more active, keen, and brilliant than it was at Saranac Lake after he had rested for a few weeks. He was often given to deep and tender reminiscences. Certainly I had never realized quite so fully his magnetic charm in quiet personal conversation as I did at that time.

Tradition has it that in the house where we were living at the Lake, Robert Louis Stevenson had sojourned for a season as a patient of the great Doctor Trudeau and that there he wrote *The Master of Ballantrae,* one of his best novels, and a noted essay, "Tahawas."

I did have a feeling then that if I but dared, I could act as amanuensis for a most interesting story of Mr. Hunton's life. But I was too anxious for his recovery to suggest taking the slightest risk. However, much that I have been able to say in this book has greater clarity and fervor because of those shining uninterrupted hours that God gave us together in that glorious setting. Our companionship through the years had been kept close during long separations by the united rhythm of our spirits; but now for the first time we were able to go on from day to day with the assurance that tomorrow would still find us near each other in person.

I think that God willed it that we should have almost three years of unbroken companionship before our earthly ties were broken. Mr. Hunton was very jealous of every moment of that time and very restless when anything took me from his side even for a brief period. I think it was as much this privilege as his desire to recover that made him perfectly amenable to any rules set for him by doctor or nurse, no matter how irksome they might be. He was very gentle, patient, tender and loving. I think that we could both say at Saranac:

> The hours of pain have yielded good
>   Which prosperous days refused,
> As herbs though scentless when entire
>   Spread fragrance when they're bruised.

Messages from the outside world, touching and encouraging, continued to reach us. In fact, if all the letters received at that time were printed, they would in themselves make a good-sized volume. Space makes it necessary to mention but a few of them. However, I do want to give one in its entirety. It came from the Right Rev. J. Albert Johnson, of the African Methodist Episcopal

Church, who was at that time in South Africa. His wife had informed him of Mr. Hunton's illness. He wrote from Capetown as follows:

My Dear Friend Willie:

I have just learned in a letter from Minnie of your illness. How serious the trouble, she does not say. It is sufficient for me to know that you are laid by. I am, indeed, sorry to hear it. Your life has been such an inspiration to the young manhood of Canada and the United States. You have, under God, set in motion so many active forces to stimulate the good in our young men. Altogether your life has been one of splendid service. We who know best, love you most, and we are assured that your calling is of God. What a comfort after all, to feel that one is not disobedient to the heavenly vision. When one is thus fully satisfied, it is easy to be always abounding in the work of the Lord, one does not labor in vain.

May the peace of God which passeth all understanding keep your heart and mind.

My own health has been indifferent for the past two years.

Of course you know that we are engaged in war here in South Africa, with the Germans on our border. Capetown is the principal base. Most of our industries are suspended, and many are in want. Still this is God's world, bought with a great price, and righteousness will finally prevail.

Rest in the Lord, wait patiently for Him, and He shall give thee thy heart's desire.

I pray for you.

From that faithful friend, Dr. Frank K. Sanders, may also be quoted these cheering words:

Do not think because you have not heard from me very recently, that I have not thought of you a great many times and hoped that your stay up in the woods was being of great service to you. I have not seen Mr. Moorland or any one who keeps in close touch with you for some time, so I am quite in the dark as to your plans. I take it for granted, however, that you will stay up there as long as it is profitable to do so, possibly all winter.

It must cheer you to know that the student work is being pushed on the whole effectively. Your guiding hand and wise head are greatly needed, and yet, real progress seems to be possible. Tobias is certainly a winner. The new man called on me the other day. I had seen him, of course, at Camp Chesa-

146

peake, but found my favorable impression renewed. We are to have a meeting in about ten days when I hope we will be able to swap chairmen and start off with new efficiency.

From President Morrow of Fisk University came these loving words:

> I am greatly delighted to learn of all the encouraging symptoms and of the strong probability that you will be able to master the disease that has come upon you so suddenly. Remember that your numberless friends are thinking of you most lovingly and praying for you most earnestly.
>
> Anticipating with joy the day when you will be strong and hearty again in the work that has been so remarkably furthered by you, I am

Mr. A. L. Parker, President of the Detroit Association, which had made such substantial contributions to the work of the Colored Men's Department, sent this message:

My Dear Hunton:

> I hope, trust and pray that you will soon be restored to health and strength again and be able to get back into the game with your old time punch and vigor.
>
> Any way you have done a whole lot of good service and lived more in the years that you have been in active service than three or four ordinary men. Believe me,

From the Chesapeake Summer School, at Arundel-on-the-Bay, came these lines from his friend and co-worker, Professor John B. Watson:

My Dear Hunton:

> We are about to close the two weeks work at Arundel and it seems that this has been a good year. But we have all missed you more than we can express. Without an exception the men have missed you. None can see fully what one means to a great cause until he is out for a while. Hurry up and shake off this thing that detains you.
>
> We had a great bunch of fellows this year. The new men are above the usual.
>
> With great love, I am glad to be
>   Sincerely yours,

147

And then came this telegram from the Summer School at its close:

> At Arundel's closing vesper service, as evening shades fell upon Bay, meadow and our lifted faces, a prayer was offered up that God might spare your life which has been for us a shining example and inspiration and to all the young men of the race. The heartfelt prayer of all your boys is that God will continue to sustain and comfort you and yours.

Besides the many letters from friends everywhere and the post-cards sent us from many vacation spots during that summer, now and then there came someone from the busy world to visit for a day or two.

But most of all I think we enjoyed those long quiet hours that were uninterrupted except by the nurse, when Mr. Hunton in his bed and with me near by, would study the daily miracle of that visible world of beauty that stretched before us. We could in our imagining give familiar forms to the precipitous and jagged peaks of the mountains and to the clouds above them. It is hardly possible to exaggerate their ever-changing beauty. At one time they were shot through with the silver rays of a glistening sun; at another time they were fiery; at still another they were ebony hued, and then suddenly silhouetted by the vivid brilliance of streaked lightning.

We somehow came to know through these mountains that it takes time to properly estimate size and space. There was Mount Marcy, seemingly at our door and possible of being easily scaled, when in reality it was miles away and more than five thousand feet high. I had lived with my children for many months in Switzerland and had seen most of its far-famed mountains and lakes from Rigi to Mt. Blanc, but we came to feel at Saranac that we had known no greater glory than that experienced in the contemplation of the mountains that were about us there.

Dr. Kinghorn desired to have Mr. Hunton under close observation for a period, and so it was decided to move him to what was known there as the Reception Hospital for the month of September. Meanwhile, I returned to Washington to look after our affairs and to Brooklyn to enter our daughter in school again.

Although I was away but a week, it was a very long week for both of us and had no good effect on my husband's mind or physical condition. He liked his little cottage very much and was very anxious to return to it, although he found the physicians at the hospital—especially Dr. Baldwin, who was in charge—nurses, and patients all very kind. He had a visit while at the hospital, of which he himself wrote me:

> About nine-thirty last night, the nurse came to my room and asked if I could see a friend of Dr. Baldwin who wanted to see me and, of course, I said yes. Then Dr. Baldwin came in with a Mr. Brainerd who had motored up from New York with him. He is the son of Mr. Cephas Brainerd who was once Chairman of the International Committee. He is just like his father who was a very good friend of mine.
>
> We had a fine chat until Dr. Baldwin announced that he would have to leave in order to make the ten-twenty train. He brought kind greetings from his sister also. His visit was a great pleasure and help to me.

Friends continued to show their interest in Mr. Hunton through letters, some serious, some humorous. Mr. C. B. Willis, General Secretary of the Milwaukee Association, wrote:

> My Dear Hunton:
>
> I am very sorry to hear that your illness continues. I had hoped to hear before now of your at least partial recovery, but I note in a copy of *Association Men* received this morning that you are still at Saranac Lake.
>
> You may rest assured, my dear fellow, that we remember you most warmly in our prayers. You made friends when you were here, who are solicitous about your welfare, and, being a friend of mine of so many years standing, I am very anxious to have you get better and be among us again. But if you have to rest for a while, I hope that you may have the patience to wait, for a good many times the dear Lord wants us to just stand and wait. That is harder, I reckon, than it is to be busy. You have probably found it out by this time.

And Mr. William D. Murray, formerly Chairman of the International Committee, wrote a letter on paper which had upon it the picture of a Puritan holding a rifle with a turkey on the ground in front of him:

My Dear Hunton:

I have a habit of writing letters with pictures in them, so I am going to try my hand on you. This is a sort of Thanksgiving day letter, somewhat ahead of time.

I had a letter from my friend Johnson, who told me that you were improving. I was indeed glad to hear it. Let us hope and pray that very soon you will be back at your splendid work.

I was at the Twenty-eighth Street building this morning and found it the usual bee hive. It always does me good to be there at the little noon prayer service. Today Jenkins told us about some of the men who are bothered by the way. . . . No one seems to be in danger, but many are inconvenienced. Mott is now in England, having visited both Paris and Berlin.

I wish you had some of my health for with all that I have to do, I seem to grow fat day by day.

My Primary Department of one hundred and fifty children gives me an hour of great joy every Sunday. One little three year old, whose father has a wooden leg, said the other day: "When I grow up I'm going to have a wooden leg like daddy." How they do look up to us, fathers and mothers.

Well, I must say good-bye.

With all good wishes.

Among others whose letters greatly cheered him were Dr. William J. Schieffelin, the Chairman of the Colored Men's Department of the Young Men's Christian Association, Mr. James Stokes, whose guest he had been in France twenty years earlier, President S. M. Newman of Howard University, and Miss Grace Dodge, Chairman of the National Board of the Young Women's Christian Associations, who died so suddenly at the end of that year. Many of the secretaries with whom he had intimate touch also wrote to him.

When I went to see him at the Reception Hospital the morning of my return from New York, he told me how he had dreamed of being near a cathedral in which beautiful music was being played and sung. He heard it all, but when he awakened could remember only a fragment that he had written and here follows:

And there all defective flowers
Will be fresh and fair and sweet;
And seared and bruised lives
Will be made perfect in His Sight.

He wrote those lines on a fly leaf of his Bible and pondered over them very often in the months that followed.

Mr. Hunton's condition was not improved at the hospital because of his great desire to be at home, so that his physician shortened his period of observation and permitted him to return to the cottage. This intense longing had provoked a slight relapse, but again he rallied quickly and looked and felt better than for many previous months. But it had been very evident at the end of September that, although he had made remarkable improvement in the three months, resting in the undisturbed quiet of an almost rural atmosphere and benefiting by its life-giving air, he was not yet beyond danger. Therefore, we set about to make ourselves as content and as comfortable as possible and to face the unusual cold of that region.

Already autumn had come and the hues of the forest were fast changing from vivid greens to orange and red with here and there a sombre contrasting tinge. Mr. Hunton was hopeful and happy as we once again took up our vigils with the mountains and witnessed their changing moods as summer gave place to winter. Across the valley was a very large mansion with many windows, which, when the sun shone against them or the house was brilliantly lighted, gave a fairy-like glamour to all the surrounding country. Mr. Hunton named it "the house of a thousand gleams."

At the beginning it had seemed to me as to others a great and terrible waste that one so spiritually and mentally fit and of such matured judgment should be removed in the very prime of life from its arena. It had not seemed quite right. But as we quietly and leisurely faced life that fall with the majesty of nature surrounding and affecting us, as we read books and discussed the characters portrayed in them, a new strength came to us that made our affliction easier to bear. It was strength in the belief that divine force or power is stronger and more vital than any activity that is the expression of it. This truth pressed home to us, not only soothed and comforted our souls, but also helped Mr. Hunton toward a greater physical ease and gain. He had been an indefatigable worker for a quarter of a century and more, so that it was not easy for him to be suddenly out of the running nor to find

151

joy in complete relaxation until this new truth had entered his mind. In many ways the mountains, inscrutable as they are, reveal not only the greatness of God but the frailty of men.

There was so much more to make us happy that fall and winter than we had been able to foresee. Our small son, Alphaeus, remained with us and was in school. His father enjoyed helping him with his studies, a privilege that he had but very rarely had with his children. Both Mr. Hunton and Alphaeus were lovers of beauty and they discovered much to evaluate and to enjoy together. Moreover, cheer and news from the outside world were brought with the precious visits of Dr. Moorland and President Hope and a few other friends who came to us at different times. Letters came very frequently as at first and were always a source of interest and comfort, and Eunice, at school in Brooklyn, wrote constantly to her father.

After the formal observance of Thanksgiving, which Mr. Hunton freely shared, we began looking forward to the coming of Christmas, which would bring Eunice to join us. She was always the most animated member of our family and kept her father cheerful. It was an unforgettable holiday that comes back each year to make us a little wistful. Mr. Hunton's room and porch were the center of all our gala festivities. He directed the decorating done by the children and entered heartily into all the preparations. There was the bright little Christmas tree on the porch, with the silvery white world without for a background. It was even more beautiful when, with only candles for light, we ate our Christmas dinner, seeing very clearly through all the dark that echelon of snow-capped peaks beyond. Mr. Hunton was weary at the close of the day, but he experienced such a sense of peace that he said that he would have liked very much to send his voice reverberating through the mountains in grateful praise.

He lived quietly but happily that winter, flooded with a joyful hopefulness and deeply appreciative of love and friendship. In his exquisite fairy-like domain he took an intense delight and called me often to witness its constantly changing beauty. Sometimes it would be to see the mountains behind a veil of falling snow or the white peaks tipped with gold by the sunset gleaming upon them.

The well-springs of his being were never richer. He found time for the assimilation of his life as he had lived it and with its whole in perspective. All the facets of his precious being were scintillating with a new lustre. He could often see very clearly what could have been better done. He even realized that he could have more adroitly controlled some of the opposing forces that strained at him as his work had grown in importance and extent. But there were no rueful regrets. He simply reviewed all in a dispassionate light.

Young William Hunton, the nephew who had visited us at the time of our arrival at Saranac Lake, died in the early fall, soon after his return to Montreal. Six weeks later his father, George Hunton, expired very suddenly. He had visited Mr. Hunton in the early days of his illness at Washington and had then gone to Saranac Lake to help plan for our life there. He had seemed to be in perfect health, but now this very dear brother was unexpectedly dead. We did not dare to tell Mr. Hunton and were able to keep the newspapers, carrying an account of the death, away from him. Nor did he suspect the truth when his brother Phillip and sister Victoria came directly from the funeral at Montreal to visit him. Now and then for a while he expressed wonder that George did not write him, but attributed it to his grief over the passing of his son. However, some time later, he asked me quite directly when and how George had died, knowing, as he said, that nothing else would have kept him silent for so long a time.

The only thing that gave him grave concern at that time was the growing conflict abroad in which Great Britain was involved. He was inherently a loyal British subject, but neither victory nor defeat elicited from him any animated comment. Seeing only waste in war, he was always an earnest advocate of peace, and at our family devotions prayed fervently for its return.

The winter finally passed. No longer did the temperature fall at times to thirty degrees below zero, although there at Saranac this had been easier to bear than a few degrees above zero in New York City. No longer were we sleeping at night with a blanket of snow atop our woolen one, shaking it off in the morning as though it were sand. The frozen lakes, dog sleds, ice palace, and carnival were all things of the past. Mr. Hunton was beginning to move about the house and grounds and to take short walks. His hope and courage now flared again, because Doctor Kinghorn had expressed his belief that he would be able to return to active life in the coming fall.

We had found food very high priced because of the distance of Saranac from the main arteries of traffic and because of its very long and severe winters. We decided upon having a vegetable garden as a measure of economy, and at the same time as a pleasurable interest. It was, our neighbors suggested, a rather daring venture, but it did prove successful beyond our dreams. Mr. Hunton very thoroughly bossed the job, while a man with a horse and plow at first, and Alphaeus and I afterwards, did the actual work. We raised not only all the vegetables we needed for our own consumption during the summer, including corn, which the natives told us could not be grown, but had some to spare for our newly made friends there. It was a very pretty garden, too, as we had planted nasturtiums between the rows of different vegetables. It had entailed some hard work, and the birds led us a merry chase by day while the frost nipped our fingers at night as we sought to protect the plants from the cold. But we had our reward, for Mr. Hunton enjoyed directing our work and walking in the garden as it developed. And furthermore, the products of our garden won two blue ribbons and a two-dollar-and-a-half gold piece at the county fair that summer. We promptly decorated the director with both blue ribbons and applied the money to the expense of a pilgrimage we were planning to make.

Our first summer at Saranac had been too perilous for Mr. Hunton to leave us any desire for rambles or adventure in that grand region and, too, we had much more loveliness at our own door than we could enjoy all at once. However, this second summer he had been able to walk and sit by the lakeside and take short drives. I left him for a few days to attend a summer conference of the Young Women's Christian Associations at Silver Bay, on

Lake George, and again one afternoon to see lovely Lake Placid and the grave of John Brown near by. He was very desirous that we should make the pilgrimage to the shrine of this martyr whose life had touched so closely that of his own father and, when we returned, he gave close attention while we tried to describe the little cemetery, the house, and every detail of that sacred spot.

Toward the end of that summer, Mr. Hunton became what seemed to us, suddenly and alarmingly ill. But his physician said that he had been rather expecting that he would have one more hemorrhage. He was again put to bed, but recovered very rapidly and was soon stronger than before. An x-ray test in early October revealed his lungs quite healed and his doctor decided that he could return to New York City without risk, although he would not be permitted to take active part in any work.

Early November, 1915, saw his face turned once more to the world he knew best and which still beckoned him—the world of Christian service.

Saranac had been to Mr. Hunton a profound experience. Always endowed with patience and always humble, he had found it necessary to bow very low before the Cross to know the full value of those two gifts. His faith had been given the stamp of the impregnable mountains; he knew now in its fullness the meaning of love, friendship, and trust; and with all, he had grown more in the likeness of the blessed Master.

Every one there whom he had touched and known had been exceptionally kind—ministers, physicians, and civic leaders had all called and invited him to participate in their affairs. The people in that little village were made very human and drawn into a close fellowship because of the common enemy that so many were fighting. Mr. Hunton went away happy and grateful.

CHAPTER TWELVE

The Last Year

SARANAC LAKE had given to Mr. Hunton a winging spirit with which to reach the pinnacle of his devotional life. But coming again into the rush and passion of a crowded existence, he had to fortify himself for the meeting of a more practical and rougher life. This return to the ordinary world would have been a most depressing one to most persons with the background of his immediate past.

It had been decided before we left Saranac Lake that he should be taken at once to a hospital on his arrival in New York. A series of serum treatments would be administered to him while we were getting our home prepared for him. The specialist chosen to treat him had selected the Polyclinic Hospital, and there he was taken. I went to visit him the first evening and found him comfortably served in a quiet room. The next evening I found him far removed to an improvised room, situated somewhere between the din of the kitchen clatter and telephone stand.

He was quiet and calm, but with no martyr's expression. He said very quickly, "Do not be angry, dear, but please get me out of this place." It was too late to attempt a change that night, but with the morning I was in touch with influential friends. Efforts were made at once to have him returned to the room he had first occupied, but they failed absolutely. As I left the hospital to search for a place where he would be both welcome and happy, I paused for a moment to re-read the sign over the portal that had so attracted me at the time of my first visit. I thought I might have been mistaken in reading its offer of welcome to those who needed healing without regard to race or creed, but I was not and could only conclude that *exclusive of colored people* was to be implied after the word "Race." We found a haven for Mr. Hunton that day, but gone were those months in that little Adirondack village. They had been like an idyll, but if he suffered in this sudden change he gave no sign. His one comment when finally settled in a quiet home was: "This is so much better!" I confess that only because of his superb calm were my feelings held in check.

Just after the foregoing incident, the country was shocked by the unexpected death of Dr. Booker T. Washington. The Sunday morning papers heralding this sad news reached Mr. Hunton before I could prevent it, and he was profoundly stirred. He had known Doctor Washington intimately for many years and had rendered much service at Tuskegee. Mr. Washington in turn had spoken again and again for his work at conventions, conferences, and parlor meetings, and during his long illness had taken time to send him assurances of sympathy and good cheer.

It may be said that Mr. Hunton was never addicted to hero worship nor was he extravagant in his praise of people and things. Just once in the many years of our constant correspondence did he write in superlative terms of anyone.

In 1899 he had written, relative of Doctor Washington, as follows:

> No man's work is perfect. Most men in prominent positions (and Mr. Washington certainly is one of them) say much that cannot be endorsed by all good people. But I cannot understand how anyone who knows the real condition and needs of our people and who knows also what Tuskegee is doing could refrain from defending Tuskegee's work against petty attacks. If Tuskegee should fail, it would be one of the greatest calamities that could befall us. If Tuskegee should fail, it would not be because of mistakes that Mr. Washington has made, but it would result from the impatience of the supporters of Tuskegee resulting from constant attacks and because of the lack of confidence in the race which such attacks are bound to inspire.

And now, some sixteen years later, when Mr. Washington had attained world-wide recognition for his labors and gone to his reward, Mr. Hunton said of him:

> His public life was not an easy one, he had far more opposition than was warranted, but he was not only a great man but a far-visioned one.

157

Doctor Washington's death and the hospital incident no doubt affected for a time his usual happy spirit, but when we were settled once more in our home with all the comforts of private life, Mr. Hunton seemed truly on the road to perfect recovery. He had changed in personal appearance very much, being clean-shaven. And as he had increased in weight from one hundred and sixty-five pounds to one hundred and ninety-five, the question of clothes was a problem now indeed. We fully realized this when, for the first time in three years, he tried to don his evening suit. It was the occasion of the memorial service for Mr. Washington held at Carnegie Hall. We were finally compelled to compromise on a Prince Albert coat.

That Christmas of 1915 was a quiet one, but with friends about us and Mr. Hunton presiding at meals, it was the most normal holiday we had experienced in several years. He was later able to go to New York two or three times a week for treatment and would frequently stop at the office of the International Committee. Aside from the memorial for Dr. Washington, he attended just one other event. It was the great athletic meet held in Brooklyn that season. We teased him by saying that he stole some honors from Howard Drew, who beat his own record that year, for when friends discovered that Mr. Hunton was in the box of Mr. and Mrs. William F. Trotman, they came from all parts of the great armory to greet him.

But he spent most of his time resting, either in bed, in his reclining chair, or in the park that fronted our home. When he sat in the park, one of the children, some friend, or I was at his side. At this period, the children had his full companionship and sympathetic help in the pursuance of their studies. He had an unobtrusive way of quickening their imaginations and of inspiring their minds.

In Brooklyn, where we lived after our return from Saranac Lake, we had no glorious panorama of mountains with elusive sunsets before us as we reasoned together, discussed books, or sat in silence, but we did have a keen sense of reality and stability, and found joy in each other's presence. We were always talking of the future and especially planning for our children. Of his own work, too, Mr. Hunton talked. His illness had brought with it the keener realization that no great movement relies for its success on any one individual. He was still eager to serve, but he also wanted to be in the van of progress and in touch with fresher minds. To him came very often his friends and colleagues and he was very glad for the definite progress being made in the Colored Men's Department of the Young Men's Christian Association. One of his most constant visitors at this time was the Rev. Robert Wheeler, who happened to be that first delegate from Howard University to a Y.M.C.A. International Convention. He had recently retired from a pastorate of many years in Hartford, Connecticut, and was making his home in Brooklyn. The Wheeler and Hunton families had been neighbors and close friends in Chatham, Ontario. Mr. Hunton grew to depend on the visits of this venerable friend, who read, prayed, and conversed with him in his own quiet way.

In the spring of 1916 we had decided that Mr. Hunton would probably be more comfortable in his own home, with access to a good park at his door, than at any other place during the coming summer, and we went forward in that belief. There had been nothing to shake our faith and hope during that winter, when very suddenly the second crisis came and, as at first, I was alone in the house with him. I had just entered his room and handed him the nourishment that he took quite regularly at eleven o'clock every morning. I turned from him for a moment, but he uttered such a cry of anguish that I whirled about to find his face distorted by a pain too great for speech. Very fortunately, I remembered some medicine given me to administer in an emergency. When he was relieved, I called our friend and family physician, Dr. James Trimble, who came very quickly. Neither Mr. Hunton nor I could talk to each other for some time; we were shaken by a great emotion for we both were somehow aware even in the moments of that terrible agony of the hopelessness of our fight. We had learned at Saranac Lake of the various forms of tuberculosis and that, of all, none was quite so impossible of cure as that of the throat. Dr. Trimble, after two or three visits to Mr. Hunton, who in the meantime had grown steadily worse, suggested that a throat specialist be called. He came, but only to confirm our fears. We did not tell Mr. Hunton the verdict, but

159

he knew. Preparation went forward for his return to Saranac Lake. However, he proved too weak for such a long trip and was instead taken to a private hospital in the suburbs of Poughkeepsie.

For the first time hope deserted him, and he said, "I am going to die and prefer to be home with you and the children." But I begged him to go for the greater comfort the climate would give him and promised to keep close to him. We spent most of our time with him through that summer, and my good friend, Mrs. M. M. Harden, opened wide the doors of her home in Poughkeepsie for the children and me.

One day in October of 1916, when I went to see him, he took my hand in his and told me very quietly but positively that he had not long to live and desired to return to the bosom of his family. I went home, made the necessary preparations, and returned to Poughkeepsie for him. Every detail had been planned for the change from the time he would be taken from his hospital bed at Poughkeepsie until he should be laid on his own at home. His sister, Victoria, and my friend, Mrs. Bauduit, who had been with me at Washington and Saranac Lake, had come to be with us again, and that other close friend, Mrs. M. B. Trotman, was ever near to comfort and to serve. With the children, we stood at his bedside while he was being comfortably settled. He scanned each of our faces closely, and with a sigh of contentment and a smile on his face, said: "Now I am satisfied." He had grown pathetically thin in body in those weeks of much agony, but his face was handsome and glowing. He was resigned in the knowledge that he was done with his earthly life and was waiting patiently for its end.

And so were we all waiting, but tense as he was not. We knew it was only a question of how long his heart could bear the strain, for the doctor was keeping him asleep much of the time. Neither Mr. Hunton nor we could endure the agony of those paroxysms of his throat. He would be very wistful at times and told me again and again that his only regret in dying was leaving the children and me alone. I had become resigned, too, through his prayers, and tried to assure him that I would bravely face the future, though I could not say I had no fear.

We lived within the shadow of death all those weeks, but, as

160

this shadow deepened, I think we had the consciousness that Mr. Hunton himself was preparing us for the end. He talked and prayed with each one of us separately and collectively. One man said of him:

> It is difficult to know Mr. Hunton and remain skeptical or indifferent to the beauty and truth of that life he so earnestly and bravely espouses.

This was especially true of him in his last hour. He had a compelling spiritual power that shamed our lesser faith and courage.

I am not embarrassed to write, nor do I make any apology for so doing, that in his death those who were at his side as well as myself saw the passing of a saint.

Wednesday morning, November 26, 1916, he made request to have some time with the children before they left for school. When they had entered his room, he asked them and me to kneel by his bedside. Placing his hand upon each head in turn, he prayed a little prayer for us. It was a precious blessing that has since that time given light to many a dark path.

Later in the morning he was given his last communion by the Rev. George Frazier Miller, D.D. As it had been necessary to administer an opiate just before Dr. Miller came, he had to make a desperate effort to retain consciousness as the rites were held. Fitfully conscious all that morning, he would pat or hold my apron as best he could and use endearing terms in an effort to comfort me. Late in the afternoon he lapsed into a coma from which he did not again arouse, and just on the eve of Thanksgiving, his visage showed that he had been beckoned by God and was at rest in the Land of Eternal Thanksgiving.

It was all so beautiful, so quiet, and yet with such a full and thrilling sweep from time into eternity that my sorrow was stilled and I could wail no monody. My desolate hour must wait. This had been Mr. Hunton's triumphant hour—the consummation of all his devotion to service and to God.

The beautiful lines below, spoken by a great man at the close of the life of the sainted Phillips Brooks, can with appropriateness be iterated here.

We thank Thee that Thou didst put into the hearts of the

people to choose such a man—so full of goodness, truth and the faithfulness—patience, serenity and composure, of such wisdom to perceive the truth and such steadfastness to do it—for the earnestness with which he laid hold upon the greater purposes of life before him in long hours of preparation.

A very quiet service took place at Mr. Hunton's home Saturday noon. It was conducted by the Rev. George Frazier Miller, and short talks were made by the Right Rev. J. Albert Johnson, who had just returned from his South African field; by Dr. Lucien C. Warner, of the International Committee of the Young Men's Christian Associations; and by Mr. Channing H. Tobias, of the staff of the Colored Men's Department, of which Mr. Hunton had been administrator for twenty-five years. The Rev. William M. Moss of Brooklyn, formerly pastor at Norfolk, Virginia, also paid tribute to Mr. Hunton. Mr. Harry T. Burleigh and Mrs. Nellie Ford Brooks sang while Association men who had gathered from every section of the country chorused Mr. Hunton's favorite hymns.

Also present at this service were representatives of the National Board of the Young Women's Christian Associations, headed by Miss Mabel Cratty, the Executive Secretary; The Brooklyn Citizen's Club; and the Northeastern chapter of the Sigma Pi Phi, of which Mr. Hunton was Archon at the time of his death.

The honorary pallbearers were Mr. Caspar Titus, of Norfolk, Virginia; the Hon. E. A. Johnson, of New York City; Drs. Roland Johnson and James Trimble, and Prof. William Bulkley and Mr. Frank Gilbert, all of Brooklyn. Secretaries of the Young Men's Christian Associations formed the active pallbearers, and the International Staff accompanied the family.

The interment was on a hillside in the beautiful Cypress Hills Cemetery, to which a pilgrimage has been made each year since by Association men—first under the leadership of Mr. Thomas E. Taylor and, since his retirement, under Mr. Henry C. Parker, Jr. My last memory of Mr. Richard C. Morse, for so many years the Executive Secretary of the International Committee of the Young Men's Christian Associations, is as I saw him standing by the grave of Mr. Hunton one very cold Sabbath morning when he was participating in a pilgrimage made to that spot by the Alpha Phi Alpha Fraternity during an annual convention that was being held in New York City.

Writing of the funeral service of Mr. Hunton, Dr. Frank K. Sanders said:

> I was very glad to attend the funeral on Saturday of your late husband who was so valued a friend to us all. I need not tell you how deeply we sympathize with you in your affliction.
>
> I was deeply interested in the splendid gathering at your house, which testified to the wide-ranging intimacies and friendships which your husband had formed. His work will not soon be forgotten. His was the creative genius that gave it form and raised up and developed a number of those who are continually adding substance to it. No one was so intimately connected with the whole progress of effective work among colored young men in institutions as he. It is a very great grief to us all that he was unable to see the fullest fruition of his labors and to give another active quarter of a century in the development of the work, but I trust that peace was in his heart as one who had done his best in glorious fashion, and had really created a form of service which will be significant for all time.
>
> Yours very sincerely and sympathetically,

Many letters came after Mr. Hunton's death, not only from those who had been co-laborers with him in Association work, but from a wide range of friends, young and old, men and women, white and colored. Only a few, indicating his far-flung influence, can be mentioned in a book of this compass. From Dr. H. H. Proctor, then a pastor in Atlanta, Georgia, came this word:

> Please accept my sincerest sympathy in this hour. I rejoice with your husband that he has entered upon his permanent spiritual relations. I sorrow with my people in the loss of so rare a man. As I said to my Church last Sunday, he stood out unique in his spiritual distinction from all other men of our race.
>
> Mrs. Proctor joins me in sincerest sympathy in best wishes to you and all the family circle.

And from President John Hope of the same city came this most interesting testimony:

> In the early days of my administration as president of Morehouse College, no man was more helpful to me than Hunton.

163

It took him only a few moments in his quiet way to give me some advice about running the school which helped me as much as any one thing that was ever said to me, and I believe that Hunton's advice to me was an indication of his own character and success. This is what he told me: "Make the boys love the College." Men followed him because they loved him first and believed in him afterwards. If they doubted his wisdom, they did what he wanted done because they believed in him and loved him, but it must be said to the credit of his mind that his judgments were almost always correct. I will not say more today, though much is in my heart. This is what I want you and the children to know, that I deeply sympathize with you not only as the friend of Hunton, but as the friend of you and I want to keep in touch with you as helpfully as I can.

From Mr. H. S. Ninde, who had been a member of the staff of the International Committee and a very dear friend of my husband, but who had retired and was living at Rome, New York, came this very loving message:

I had been hoping against hope for some time as I heard unfavorable accounts of the invalid's condition, but such happenings are always sudden. Mr. Hunton was on the International force a short time before myself, although I was many years his senior, and I speak with sincerity when I say that there was no man of the number for whom I had a more genuine regard. He was one of the truest of men—a thorough gentleman, efficient and one of the most sweet-tempered Christians I ever knew. Not in the least do I mourn for the change that has come to him. God has a greater work for him to do and has called him to it in His own good time. With you and your children I sympathize most heartily for your loss is irreparable, and you better than any one of us who also loved him, knew his worth and feel fully the vacancy made by his going away. But he is not far away. We shall not know less in that other world, and I feel that those we love—and lose a while—still love and care for those who were so dear to them in the earthly life. The time of separation will not be long; there will be a glorious re-union never to be broken again. May the Saviour—Will's Saviour and also yours—keep you in His own peace and comfort you with a great comfort.

And these words came from Mr. W. H. Tinker, of the

Student Department of the Young Men's Christian Association:

> My dear Mrs. Hunton:
>
> I was so distressed when the sad news of your great loss reached me. I have known Mr. Hunton so well, and Mrs. Tinker and I have had the pleasure of entertaining him in our home at Ann Arbor, Michigan.
>
> He was such a tower of strength in Association circles and such a genuine Christian. God must have had a lot of urgent and important work for him to do in the home above or he could not have called him so soon from his work here. You will miss him terribly I know, but the comfort of a great faith will sustain you during even the hardest days.

Mrs. Booker T. Washington, with her own recent loss still deeply poignant, wrote:

> I am in the country or I would have come to you immediately. I am here under treatment and was so nervous that I simply had to get out of the city.
>
> I have been told that the funeral was today. I do not think that I *can come now*. I simply *cannot*. It is all too terrible for me. Forgive me if I seem a coward, but I cannot bring myself to see you, my dear friend. How empty life is now for us.

Then a more cheerful word came from the Chicago Metropolitan staff, written by Mr. William J. Parker:

> The sterling character as well as the splendid service of your husband endeared him to all of us who knew him.
>
> His spirit remains in the work to which he gave so many years. His great work lives after him and will continue to reflect credit upon him who guided it in its formative period. I have never had the pleasure of meeting you, but am sure that you will regard my years of acquaintance with Mr. Hunton as giving me liberty to write this letter. You have suffered a great loss, but you have the great comfort of knowing that his life was devoted to a very worthy cause. He did his duty to his Master faithfully and with signal ability. He left this priceless heritage to you and your children.

Letters continued to come for many months, especially from foreign lands. Four months after Mr. Hunton's death, a letter was received from Shanghai. It was written by Mr. Willard

D. Lyon, one of the secretaries of the National Committee of the Young Men's Christian Associations in China, and said:

> Notification has just reached me of the passing away of your husband last November. Though late, I feel that I must send you my word of sincere sympathy. Mr. Hunton had already been in the service of the International Committee four years when I was called in 1895 to come to China. I had gotten well acquainted with him during the two preceding years when I was working for the Student Volunteer Movement and came to think very highly of him indeed. He was always so sane and at the same time so deeply spiritual that I looked at him as an unusually all-'round man. I have enjoyed all later opportunities that I have had of being with him—all too few and far between. My life is the richer for having known him. I am glad too that I have had the privilege of meeting you. I shall be the better able to help you carry your burden of sorrow. Mrs. Lyon joins me in warmest sympathy.

Many fine tributes came from student and city Associations all over the country, from members of the Southern Sociological Society and the American Academy of Political and Social Sciences, with both of which he was affiliated, and from various fraternities and organizations. However, since it is not possible to include in this book all of them, I refrain from the printing of any part of them. Perhaps, after all, they represent in their totality the greatest expression of appreciation, admiration, and devotion for William Alphaeus Hunton that could be garnered. I could wish that in some way they might be handed down to future generations. They indicate the path of a great soul as it made its way to and fro over the earth. They tell us too that his fine humility and innate sense of propriety never permitted him to essay to dominate a lesser soul. These testimonials most strikingly reveal how he always held high before him the banner of Christian idealism, never letting it droop because of any self-aggrandizement or petty fears. After two decades since his passing, men are still emphasizing these truths about him. His life was true and simple, retiring yet energetic, full of warmth and loyalty. These are the traits, we are told, that distinguish a really great character. Those testimonials proclaim that greatness, but I love best to think of him as a great *gentleman* and as saying with another lovely soul:

The human heart is all I need
    For I have found God ever there;
Love is the one sufficient creed
    And comradeship the purest prayer.

Mr. Hunton lived just a little more than a half century, but he was more fortunate than some who die thus early. He was permitted to see the beginning at least of the fulfillment of many of his dreams. He had sought to bring to the men of his race what Prof. Ralph Harlow calls the Christ in one of his exquisite poems—a "young and fearless prophet"—and because he dared he also achieved. He had seen the staff of the Colored Men's Department of the Young Men's Christian Association develop from just his own feeble but consecrated service till, at the time of his death, seven very earnest and able secretaries were carrying on "In His Name." He had seen work for boys and county organizations begun and he had seen Max Yergan depart with the message of salvation to India.

Again and again we had talked about Africa. He had a pile of letters and literature relative to that great continent. He purchased and read more books on that one single subject than any other. As early as 1894 he was in touch with an Association at Cape Palmas, and all through the years of his active life, any address that he made carried with it a fervent plea for the extension of the Young Men's Christian Association movement to African territory. I think his last petition, had he made one, would have been but an echo of that made by David Livingstone in his last lonely hours in Africa—for the evangelization of that vast and strategic land. Mr. Hunton's pleas, prayers, and visions for Africa found their fulfillment in the splendid efforts of that new pioneer prophet, Max Yergan, who entered that mysteriously ageless land by the way of South Africa, bearing the banner of the Young Men's Christian Association. The symbol of this banner proclaims healing for body, mind, and spirit.

The tasks to which Mr. Hunton had been called to devote his energies were finished, so far as his part was concerned, before this

167

country was swept into that terrible cataclysm that men named the
World War. His sensitive soul was spared the anguish involved
in a struggle to hold fast to cherished ideals and inherent loyalties.
He was not made to witness the violation and, in some cases, the
destruction of the fundamental principles of truth and justice.
Who knows what reaction upon his spirit the tragic happenings of
that difficult period might have had, had he lived!

Let us rejoice rather that he died at the end of an old order—
died a shining light that the faith and courage of some men might
not be lost in utter darkness and that the leaders of the Young
Men's Christian Association movement might still see their way to
a new honor and a new glory in a new age.

Truth was more to him than a world beside—
That one foundation did all else sustain.

Essential Portions of a Memorial Address

on

William A. Hunton

By

FRANK K. SANDERS

I REALIZE that I am paying tribute to Mr. Hunton on behalf of his colleagues in that work, for the *committee* of the department which he created in large measure, for the *International Committee* of Young Men's Christian Associations whose members listened to his pleas with rapidly growing interest and enthusiasm, and for the *Brotherhood* throughout the country and the world who have looked upon him, as the living embodiment of the cause he championed at conventions and meetings with matchless eloquence and insight. In a work so great as this movement for the young men of all lands it is always true that a few men stand out as leaders, known well by hundreds with whom they may never have had contact, representing in a peculiar way the ideals and the spirit of the cause they champion.

I recall a state convention in a western city at which for some reason Mr. Hunton and his work were sidetracked. No one in responsible charge of the program knew him, because the state had not been on his schedule. He came to me to state the facts and to ask how he could get even a brief opportunity to address the convention. I was to preside at the closing session and assured him that if he would appear at a certain time I would introduce him for just ten minutes. He followed the advice and in that ten minutes made an address so moving, so illuminating, so gracious, so thrilling that the audience cheered him to the echo, expressed their approval of his plea, and remembered him for life.

No man can be fairly judged on the mere record of his yearly activity, nor does the significance of the service he has rendered appear through the recital of what he has brought about. One man is active every moment of his life but is at best little more than a small cog in the speeding wheel of social efficiency; another sits quietly at a desk, doing apparently no strenuous work, yet in reality determining the destinies of thousands. Viewed from the personal angle alone Mr. Hunton may not have achieved as many tasks as some others might have accomplished, for he did not bustle about. He was rather of the quiet, thoughtful, interpreting temperament. He would have made an ideal member of a college faculty, had God not called him to a work no less significant and more unique.

But neither can we estimate our brother merely on his working record during the quarter of a century which he gave so wholeheartedly to the Young Men's Christian Association movement in this country. He was an active agent; he handled large undertakings; he negotiated many a delicate situation; he was widely trusted; his leadership was acknowledged by all, and yet the greater significance of his work is only to be seen as we survey it historically in the larger setting of the half century or more which has elapsed since the Civil War. That conflict settled one great problem and created several. It gave freedom to the Negro race, but it did not give them that national consciousness, those social and intellectual standards, that fine community life which develops true citizenship and absolute dependableness. The acquisition and the dissemination of these elements has been a slow gradual process in which the Young Men's Christian Association, with its traditions of democracy and brotherhood, its many-angled appeal to manhood and boyhood, its growing share in social movements of all kinds, and its lofty religious spirit and high standards of living, has taken no unimportant share. With the pioneering stages of the development of the work of young men for young men among the colored race in North America Mr. Hunton's name will always be associated. No statelier monument to his memory will ever be needed than this remarkable and rapidly growing branch of the Young Men's Christian Association Movement of North America. He served his generation nobly, but he had the proud privilege of marking out lines of development whose full evaluation only time can discover.

In estimating such a work as that which Mr. Hunton developed we need to go back to its beginnings. You will bear with me, if I recount details with which many may be familiar, in order that we may see the forces which were preparing the way for him, many years ago. Mr. Hunton was not only getting ready for a unique and all-important service, but the agency which he was to direct with such consummate skill was likewise being slowly fashioned for his use.

For ten years after the close of the Civil War no attempt was made by the Young Men's Christian Association Movement on behalf of colored young men. There was held an International Convention at Richmond in 1875, at the invitation of Colonel Mumford and Major Robert Stiles, both Confederate soldiers and men of professional standing. It was the first convention held in the South after the war.

Two things happened at that meeting which from our standpoint today may be regarded as epochal in importance. The New England delegates had a Massachusetts man as their candidate for President, R. K. Remington of Fall River. But with his customary shrewdness of judgment Mr. McBurney realized the unwisdom of such a step, and secured the hearty election of Mr. Joseph Hardie of Selma, Ala., a Christian Southerner of fine character and great-hearted temperament. While he was in the chair a petition was sent in by the colored clergy of Richmond asking for the prayers of the convention on behalf of the colored young men of that city. Mr. Hardie himself led the great gathering in an earnest prayer for their interests. This convention enlisted him in a definite and fruitful participation in the work of the Associations in the Southland which has been almost to this day a factor of great importance to the specific work for colored young men.

The other occurrence was of more importance than the enlistment of a friendly Southern supporter, significant as that was, for it paved the way for the whole development of the work of the Colored Men's Department of the International Committee. A delegate presented himself with proper credentials from Howard University. The local committee at first ruled against his recognition, but others demanded that his credentials be approved, and at last he was admitted and the question of recognizing the colored race was forever set at rest, as far as International Conventions are concerned.

The next year (1876), at Toronto, where Russell Sturgis of Boston, that princely Christian layman, was presiding and Sir George Williams of London was an honored guest, another step forward was taken at Mr. Hardie's initiative. He rose in the convention and moved that the International Committee be instructed to put a man into the field to work for colored young men. Stuart Robinson of Philadelphia—a man who had been so thoroughly in sympathy with the South that he was forced during the war to leave his home and live in Canada—seconded the motion and offered $50 toward a special expense fund. Sir George Williams rose to offer $100 and from that moment the work was definitely in sight.

But there was still a long road to travel before the efficient organization of the Colored Men's Department of today could even be conceived. It was not unnatural that the International Committee should follow at first the advice of its own Southern members. They suggested the employment of General Johnston to exploit the new scheme among the white people of the South, feeling sure that he could get their approval. He was not a failure, but it was soon apparent to Mr. Hardie that the General could not get near the colored young men on whose behalf the work was supposed to be developing. The right man, however, was not easily found. But in 1879 the Committee found Henry Brown, who had been a student at Oberlin when Lincoln was assassinated. When the President's funeral train went through Oberlin, a solemn memorial service was held in the village at which President Finney, that great-hearted man of God, prayed such a prayer on behalf of the Negro race just emancipated that young Brown went back to his room, fell upon his knees and dedicated himself to the work of Christ for the colored race. He naturally entered the service of the American Missionary Association. He was the man who organized the school at Talladega, which is today a college and seminary of first-rate standing and wide-ranging influence. Mr. Brown was unassuming but very able. He approved

172

himself to colored and white people alike, so that Mr. Hardie and his associate, Mr. Lovelace of Selma, united in recommending him to the Committee in New York as an ideal field secretary for the work among colored men. With Mr. Brown's work began a real era of the getting together of North and South, and of the southern white and the southern Negro. Behind him were these splendid white men with their friendly personalities and their purses. Mr. Hardie, we have been told, died a poor man, but during his life he gave away a quarter of a million in Christian service.

From 1879 to 1887 Brown did lonely, wheel-horse work, organizing occasionally, but encouraging, teaching and studying needs. He could go, after all, only a limited way into the real problem, because he was in conflict with our fundamental Young Men's Christian Association principle that each group or class or race of men can best be reached by its own type of men. The work was waiting for the right man.

Mr. Hunton was born in Canada, but he was the son of a man who had known the bitterness of slavery, and made his house at Chatham, Ontario, a station of the underground railroad. With traditions of service he was familiar from his youth. Educated to be a teacher Mr. Hunton was called into the service of the Canadian government as a clerk in the Department of Indian Affairs at Ottawa. There he became actively interested in the work of the Young Men's Christian Association, identifying himself particularly with Bible class work and with the work for boys.

In 1887 Mr. Ingersoll, then just about concluding his great work as a railroad secretary of the International Committee, was in Ottawa on some errand and met Mr. Hunton. He came back to New York and said to Mr. Morse, "I've found a man for Brown." It was not long before Mr. Hunton was looked over and given a call at the age of twenty-five to undertake the secretaryship of the Colored Young Men's Christian Association at Norfolk, Va. His first impulse was to reject the offer, since it meant for him the exchange of a secure position for an experiment, the substitution of a social standing which was attractive for a position of more or less certain ostracism and misinterpretation, the exchange of a position allowing abundant time for the intellectual work so dear to him for one almost preventing such careful culture. It was a great struggle through which this scholarly, quiet, thoughtful man had to go. He took his case to God in prayer for a day, then returned to his visitors with the words "It is settled; I will go." Notwithstanding the united opposition of his pastor and of his intimate friends, he took up the work at Norfolk in the fall of 1888 as the first City Association General Secretary of his race.

At Norfolk Mr. Hunton had no easy task. His constituents were wholly unacquainted with Association principles and methods. But he had boundless patience, much tact and that true brotherliness which overcame all obstacles. In two years he had won the esteem of all citizens, white and colored, as few men have been able to do it, before or since. While at Norfolk he rendered occasional service to the International Committee in the extension of the work of the Association among colored young men in other cities. His work was so satisfactory that in 1890 he received a call to become the first Secretary of the Colored Men's Department of the International Committee and accepted it.

Mr. Hunton's work since then for almost a quarter of a century needs no review. It was a pioneering task, crowded with discouragements. He occasionally mentioned them only to declare that when he looked back a few years or thought of the things that surely were to be, his courage returned and he went ahead again. He was privileged to see five important achievements within these years, any two of which would have justified his leadership.

First of all, he left behind him a well-organized staff of brother workers, capable of promoting efficiently the interests of the work he loved, each one a specialist of ability, college-bred and experienced.

Secondly, he left behind him more than a hundred student Young Men's Christian Associations. To these, after he was joined by his colleague, Dr. Moorland, who took the city Associations, he gave his whole attention. Ten thousand hand-picked students, sure to be the leaders of the race—these were his jewels.

Again, he came to the deliberate conclusion that the practice, adopted at the outset of his service, of organizing colored Associations in the cities as independent organizations was a mistake. Under his leadership and that of Dr. Moorland the policy was adopted of making such Associations regular branches of the general city Associations. Under this latter policy much progress has been made in securing the co-operation of the white Association leaders and white citizens, both North and South.

Of even greater significance did he count the co-operation received from his brother white secretaries in the South, especially those identified with the extension of Association work among the white students of the South. He believed in the assured results for his people of this co-operation of the educated men of both races under strong leadership. He was sure that it would not fail to develop the sympathetic backing which is the great need of the work in the Southland.

And, finally, it was our brother's privilege in the last months of his life to learn of the appointment in Virginia by the State Committee of the first colored field secretary, a result of which he would hardly have dared to dream, ten years ago.

He would have been the first to rejoice in the splendid series of finely equipped buildings which through the far-sighted generosity of Julius Rosenwald are making possible a new and more efficient type of Association work for colored young men. But these were not, I suppose, primarily due to Mr. Hunton, except in the important sense that the splendid work which he had so much of a share in building inspired the confidence which made possible such generosity.

Such were the achievements of the short life of this one man. Measured by them his life was both long and great. Can we not see in its details the secret of its power?

Mr. Hunton was a man of rare natural gifts. He would have made a notable educator. He was an impassioned orator of unusual dignity and power on themes which stirred his soul.

But his greatest gift was his Christlike character. He left home and country and took upon himself, like his Master, the form of a servant in a Jim Crow country. He did not like the conditions under which he had to travel and to live. His whole soul revolted at times and with propriety, yet he summoned his courage, he took counsel with God, and persisted, only at the end to die a martyr to these conditions, one who gave his life deliberately for his people.

175

Mr. Hunton mastered the despondency toward which his finely organized nature tended in view of the difficulties he faced because he was a man of spiritual vision. That gave him patience, dependableness, poise, truthfulness. It gave him a mastery over all difficulties and a steadily increasing grasp of the conditions of his work. It caused him to invest every atom of energy in the extension of the Kingdom of Christianity among young men. It made him a leader who stamped his sincere, simple, beautiful and brotherly life upon thousands of the choicest among the young men of today.

He was a man of prayer, whose words always revealed his happy harmony with his Heavenly Father. He built his spiritual life upon the devotional study of the Bible. It was his daily source of strength. He translated its power into many lives other than his own.

We cannot but rejoice in the life of our brother. He did his work well. Our memorial to him will be, not new Associations, not even new buildings, but our sincere dedication to the great unfinished tasks, social, religious and racial, to which he gladly gave his life.